ESSAYS BY DIVERS HANDS:

BEING THE TRANSACTIONS OF THE ROYAL SOCIETY OF LITERATURE

New Series: Volume XLIII

ESSAYS BY DIVERS HANDS

being the transactions of
the Royal Society of Literature,
New Series: Volume XLIII

EDITED BY SIR ANGUS WILSON CBE, CLit, FRSL

Published for
the Royal Society of Literature
by the Boydell Press

© *1984 Contributors*

First published in 1984 by the Boydell Press,
an imprint of Boydell & Brewer Ltd, PO Box 9,
Woodbridge, Suffolk IP12 3DF

British Library Cataloguing in Publication Data
Essays by Divers hands being the transactions of
the Royal Society of Literature.
    New Series. Vol. 43
    1. English Literature – History and criticism
    periodicals
    I. Wilson, Angus, 1913–
    II. Royal Society of Literature
    820.9   PRI

ISBN 0-85115-407-7

Photoset in Great Britain by
Rowland Phototypesetting Ltd, Bury St Edmunds, Suffolk
and printed by St Edmundsbury Press
Bury St Edmunds, Suffolk

CONTENTS

INTRODUCTION ix
by Sir Angus Wilson CBE, CLit, FRSL

Katya Reissner Memorial Lecture
1. ROYAL ENGLISH 1
by Beatrice White, DLit, FRHistS, FSA, FRSL

Joseph Bard Memorial Lecture
2. THE CHILDREN'S WRITER: ARTIST OR TEACHER'S
   AID 17
by Geoffrey Trease, FRSL

Tredegar Memorial Lecture
3. J J ROUSSEAU AND THE BIRTH OF ROMANTICISM 34
by Maurice Cranston, FRSL

Wedmore Memorial Lecture
4. THE LIFE AND EARLY DEATH OF GEORGIANISM 47
by Samuel Hynes, FRSL

Don Carlos Coloma Memorial Lecture
5. THE HAUNTED BOOKS OF GEORGE GISSING 62
by Gillian Tindall, FRSL

Stephen Graham Memorial Lecture
6. HARDY'S WESSEX 75
by Desmond Hawkins, OBE, FRSL

Giff Edmonds Memorial Lecture
7. SHAW AND BIOGRAPHY: THE UNWRITTEN LIFE 90
by Michael Holroyd, FRHistS, FRSL

8. *Giff Edmonds Memorial Lecture*
   BEATRICE WEBB: THE NOVELIST WHO
   NEVER WAS
   by Norman Mackenzie, FRSL   104

9. *Joseph Bard Memorial Lecture*
   BOILING BELLOC
   by A N Wilson, FRSL   117

10. *Tredegar Memorial Lecture*
    OSCAR WILDE AND LORD ALFRED DOUGLAS
    by H Montgomery Hyde, DLit FRSL   139

NOTES ON MEMORIAL LECTURES

Joseph Bard   Founded in 1978 by Eileen Agar, widow of Joseph Bard who was a Fellow of the Society and Member of Council from 1946 until his death in 1975.

Joyce Brown   Founded in 1978 to honour the memory of Miss G. J. Brown who was a member and benefactor of the Society.

Don Carlos Coloma   Founded in 1964 under the will of Miss Olga Turner who was a Member of the Society and Spanish scholar, to honour the memory of Don Carlos Coloma, Spanish author.

Willard Connely   Instituted in 1967 with a legacy from Willard Connely who was a Fellow of the Society from 1943 to 1967 to provide a lecture every three years on an American subject to be given by an American.

Giff Edmonds   Founded in 1929 by Miss Sophie Gifford Edmonds, a Member of the Society, in memory of her brother Lt Nicholas Gifford Edmonds of the Black Watch, who died at Magersfontein on 11 December 1899.

Katya Reissner   Founded in 1952 by Alexander Reissner, a Member of the Society, in memory of his mother, Katya Reissner, a musician and lover of literature.

Tredegar   To perpetuate the memory of the first Viscount Tredegar. It was founded by his son, a Fellow of the Society from 1928 to 1949.

Wedmore   Endowed in memory of Sir Frederick Wedmore, author and critic, by his daughter, Millicent Wedmore, a Member of the Society from 1928 to 1964.

Stephen Graham Founded in 1980 under the will of Mrs Vera Graham to perpetuate the memory of her husband who was a Fellow of the Society from 1950 to 1975.

INTRODUCTION

Do all those who edit the volumes of Essays by Divers Hands find themselves, as I have, detecting shapes and trends within the fine diversities and varied riches which these assembled lectures offer to readers? I do not know. In the past I have been an addicted reader of the volumes, but my memory is largely of individual and very diverse essays that have set me thinking in new directions or, to be honest, also delighted me by confirming my opinions. Now, in editing this volume, I have found myself fascinated and held by a sense of directions and patterns that seem to show through almost all the ten essays contained in this book.

Two trends communicate themselves to me in the present volume. And are themselves easily connected. First, most of the lectures are directing their attention to literary movements or literary figures of a period of fifty years, roughly from the eighteen seventies to the end of World War I. Secondly, there is much concern with the vital place of the romantic imagination in literature and the danger to writers of a life that denies it, and the equal danger of an over-simplified acceptance of its images and language.

Only Beatrice White's fascinating 'Royal English' stands quite apart from the two connecting trends. After a splendid salute to Alfred's care for the English language, Professor White reminds us that from the Conquest until, at least, Henry VIII, few of our Kings spoke much English. It is all the more dramatic then when in 1381 the fourteen year old Richard II nips the Peasants' Revolt in the bud by a bold address to the rebels in the vernacular. After that, our monarchs have been variously adept in English speech, although we have a lapse in the reigns of the first two German speaking Georges. Beatrice White chronicles the differences in the English speech style of most of our monarchs. There is much magnificence of words, some frightening thunder, and more than one sort of wit. But, perhaps the most impressive is the pioneer remark of James I: 'And I would advise you to write in your own language. For there is nothing left to be said in Greek or Latin.' There is something about this royal remark that would have seemed suspiciously near blasphemy even two centuries later to, say, Dr Arnold of Rugby. We who now write in English must be grateful that England had so wise and prophetic a fool for her ruler.

Only two of the lectures in this book do not fit into the 1880–1920 time span. Mr Geoffrey Trease's, 'The Childrens' Writers: Artists or Teachers Aid?' bring knowledge and much wit to a subject very close to my heart, for although not a critic of books for children, I have for a decade or more taught the development of the treatment of children in the English novel and the two subjects are closely allied. Mr Trease succinctly narrates the moralising stranglehold that almost killed books for children after the days of the early eighteenth century pioneer, Newberry, until late Victorian England, when pure adventure and entertainment pushed out moralising, but without substituting anything serious in its place. The reign of Henty, though better than that of the Fairchild Family, dominated a great area of books for boys until recently and, it has to be said, kept the intelligence and imagination in childrens' books to a minimum (save, of course, for the great childrens' books among which Mr Trease names to my delight, *Rewards and Fairies*). In concluding passages of great concern to contemporary writers and critics, he puts the case for drawing childrens' literature into much deeper streams of creative imagination, without letting it be drowned in the waves of contemporary educational causes. This would, as he says, surely be a death for the fancy as threatening as any of the endless moralising that came near to freezing the childs' imagination in the days of Mrs Trimmer or *Sandford and Merton*.

It was this sort of moralising, of course, that made Rousseau advise that no books save *Robinson Crusoe* should be given to Emile. And when we remember the appalling diet of heavy moralising that many of Rousseau's English disciples like Edgworth fed to children we may think that he was right. Professor Maurice Cranston's 'Rousseau and the birth of Romanticism' makes a brilliant case for the too often travestied author of *Emile* in our dangerously technologised, ultra-scientific age. It is to me especially exciting for the light it sheds on the debt of music to Rousseau in his battle with Rameau in favour of the Italian opera buffa—one of his central contributions to the Encyclopedie. As Professor Cranston shows, this musical contribution, splendid in itself, goes much deeper, to that side of romanticism which insisted on the liberation of the human heart. How his political theory made full demand on man's self-discipline he also demonstrates. Given all the easy farce that has been made out of Rousseau's life, Professor Cranston's depiction of the depth and balance of his contribution to society is most well-timed, especially as Mr Gradgrind's grim shadow seems disturbingly each day to darken the sheets of our newspapers a little more.

The search for the key to the powers of romanticism and the definition of its meaning (added, no doubt, to the current and predictable reaction against the so long worshipped Modernist movement) accounts for the chronological emphasis in these many diverse essays. Indeed, it is almost stated in the title of Mr Samuel Hynes's study of Edward Marsh's now almost forgotten books of Georgian Poetry. Marsh saw 1912 as the re-birth of poetry, but the War and the new poets put an end to his anthologies in 1922 (the year of *The Waste Land* and of *Ulysses*). As Mr Hynes suggests, the ordinary man went on for a long time (until now) seeing poetry as Marsh had, but growing sophistication and university-studied literature needed something more intellectual than Masefield and Brooke.

This conflict between the 'romantic' and the 'real' can be found here in other studies of individual writers. Gillian Tindall, who has done so much to bring Gissing to our notice without ever exalting him beyond his dues, shows how seldom he found life except through the books he read. Books were his life even through three marriages. *New Grub Street* was surely his bringing alive of the other readers who surrounded him each day as he sat in the British Museum Reading Room, cut off from life. His whole life had been distorted from his college days when he set out to reclaim a prostitute and went, as a result to prison for theft. It is hard to think of his hero, Dickens, who 'did' so much for fallen women, allowing romance and reality to become so confused.

A very different marriage of romance and reality is given to us by Mr Desmond Hawkins' account of the growth of Hardy's Wessex. Starting from 1874, the publication of *Far From the Madding Crowd*, Hardy identifies himself ever more deeply with the exultation of man's rural loneliness, until as he himself said of Turner's water colours, 'each is a landscape *plus* a man's soul.' We have arrived at Tess and Jude. Wessex even today carries with it the aura of the coming together of place and the human spirit. Romanticism (Wordsworth's voice) speaks in new accents and still lives.

It is, of course, quite dead in even the first works of Bernard Shaw. As I look back and think of the enormous excitement that I received in adolescence and young manhood from the brilliant interplay of ideas, the verbal dexterity, the extraordinary theatrical shapes of the plays of Shaw that won me to going to the theatre, I also remember my growing disillusion, my deepening distaste for brilliance in which human love and sexual feeling both seemed to have been reduced to the fake flirtatiousness of an ageing mother and an indifferent son. Mr Holroyd's brilliant account of Shaw's sad early life and the emotional effect it had upon him (and through this, ultimately, upon the realism of his sparkling intellectual ideas) is a marvellous explanation of what went wrong. 'Intellectually,' Mr Holroyd says, Shaw 'travelled everywhere, emotionally he stayed at home'. Nowhere is romanticism more dead. Mr Holroyd makes me avid for his biography of Shaw. His suggestion that Shaw's fear of his own life hampers his biographers even today is a sad and menacing final note.

Professor Mackenzie suggests with some conviction that Beatrice Webb's massive diaries, too, suggest that the failure of her early passion for Chamberlain and her subsequent marriage to Sidney Webb lost us a good imaginative novelist. Romance once more was defeated in those years. I doubt myself that her novels would have substituted for her part in creating LSE and the New Statesman, however much these may be the villains in today's play. Perhaps her refusal to share her husband's elevation to the peerage—'Mrs Sidney Webb said I *will* be a pleb'—may be seen as a last romantic self dramatisation.

A more complex figure, indeed a very complex figure who nevertheless partakes of some of the unresolved interplay of Romanticism and the intellect, is surely Hilaire Belloc. Mr A. N. Wilson's lecture about him, 'Boiling Belloc' is a delight of subtlety and learning intermixed. Right radicalism was the direction of many minds in the pre-1914 wars—a mixture of the refusal of Lloyd George practical grubbiness and the half-refusal of Asquithian or Balfour-like sparkling, witty intellect. Belloc, like many a man raised in wealth to fall into deep poverty, had no sense of reality. Mr Wilson wonderfully recounts his failure to see that he had thrown an All Souls fellowship away by his tactlessness at a decisive college dinner and his failure as an MP was an equally unconscious self-destruction. His romanticism surely led him into paranoid paths, and when a friend suggested this, he attributed the suggestion to the man's Jewish blood. But he is a more complex figure than the others, for his final loyalty to his French and European Catholic origins gave him a different base both of romanticism and of realism, and his ironic wit survived separately enough to win him invitation to Clouds and friendship of the Souls—bastions which were to some degree the headquarters of the romantic movement of the 1900 to 1918 world.

Finally we have Mr Montgomery Hyde's essay on Wilde and Douglas which only marginally touches upon this whole scene. Yet if ever there was an affaire which has been seen (when not outlawed) as the height of romance it is this friendship which ultimately brought Wilde to trial and Douglas perhaps to penury. But as Mr Montgomery Hyde shows in a talk based on dogged research and conversation with sixty year old Alfred Douglas in 1931, there was never a substantial romance there, only a muddle of misunderstandings, jealousies by Wilde's other friends, and, above all, uncomprehending, injudicious actions by both men. Lord Alfred, for all his good intentions, surely wholly mistook romance for real life. In 1931 I met Lord Alfred Douglas at a party given after a performance of 'The Importance of Being Earnest', played at Westminster School, in which I, a seventeen year old schoolboy, acted Miss Prism. I sat next to this aged Apollo, one of my great romantic heroes. Thrilled, I asked him what I felt to be the right question—'Did not Mr Wilde, Sir, believe that Shakespeare's heroines should be acted by boys?' Clearly irritated, he answered, 'Very likely,' and then gave me a list of the horses who had won the races at, I think, Lingfield that day. It was just the (to me) utterly boring information that I sadly knew my Father would be quick to tell me when I returned home later that night.

ANGUS WILSON

ROYAL ENGLISH

BEATRICE WHITE DLit, FRHistS, FSA, FRSL

Read 18 November 1982:
S. Gorley Putt, OBE, FRSL, in the Chair

THE words Royal English suggest to me the use of our common vernacular by privileged and very special people, whose speech and writings, according to their various abilities, illustrate the immense potentialities of our living language.

All I hope to do this evening is to bring to your notice, with the minimum of analysis, the use of the English language as it has been spoken and written by our kings and queens. I shall begin with the greatest of them all—King Alfred, soldier, statesman, and jurist. Not only did he succeed, by brilliant tactics and clever strategy, in delivering his country from savage invasion, but he found time, even in the midst of his military and naval campaigns, to care for the education of his people. Assisted by scholars, he took those works of Latin writers that he considered essential to the welfare of capable young freemen and translated them into the vernacular.

These works range from the *Pastoral Care* of St Gregory to the *Soliloquies* of St Augustine of Hippo, and take in, by the way, the *Consolation of Philosophy* of Boethius, and the *World History* of the Spanish priest Orosius. The *Dialogues* of St Gregory were translated at Alfred's request by Werferþ, Bishop of Worcester, and the Anglo-Saxon version of the Latin *Ecclesiastical History* of St Bede was also part of his educational plan and may be attributed to his Mercian helpers. Moreover, he encouraged the chroniclers to record in the vernacular with especial detail the stirring events of his brave campaigns against the Danes.

King Alfred was no slavish translator. He never hesitated to adapt his originals to his own purpose by interpolations through which we can trace the workings of his eager intellect. We hear too, the firm tones of his voice in the basic speech rhythms of the Anglo-Saxon prose, as he gives instructions to his bishops, questions the travellers, Norwegian Ohthere, and English Wulfstan, and finds, without bungling or undue periphrasis, the apposite word for his meaning. He established Anglo-Saxon prose as an articulate, flexible literary medium, capable of expressing not only observable facts, but abstract ideas, a prose both economical and suggestive. Absorbed in his studies and plans for educational reform, he seems, as he says, to be 'looking down upon the storms of this world even as the eagle does when he soars in stormy weather above the clouds where no storm can reach him'.

King Alfred thought him 'a very foolish man and inexcusable (swiðe dysig mon and unlaede) who will not increase his knowledge while he is in this world'. And he carefully fulfilled his sincere and modest declaration:

'Þaet is me hraðost to secganne þaet ic wilnode weorþfullice to libbanne þe hwile þe ic lifde, and aefter minum lifum þaem monnum to laefanne þe aefter me waeren min gemynd on godum weorcum.' (To be brief, I desired to live honourably while I lived, and after my life to leave to the men who were after me a memorial of me in good works.)

The last lines of the poem *Beowulf* provide his aptest epitaph:

cwaedon þaet he waere	wyruldcyning(a)
manna mildust	ond monðwaerust
leodum liðost	ond lofgeornost

   (They said that he was the mildest of men and the most gentle, kindest to his people and the most eager for praise.)
'Þaet waes ʒod cyning': He was a mighty king.

Alfred was the first and last purely English king to speak and write in his native language and leave it greatly enriched. His successors were Danes, Normans, Plantagenets (both Lancastrians and Yorkists), Welsh Tudors, Scottish Stuarts, and German Hanoverians. After 1066 the English vernacular was kept alive by the common people and by the Church which, in the thirteenth century, instructed all priests to expound *in English* the main points of the Faith four times a year. The invading Normans were simply indifferent to the language of the English masses and the only post-Conquest vernacular encouraged by our early Norman and Plantagenet kings was French, that is, Anglo-Norman. That is hardly to be wondered at, considering their French wives, and their vast French possessions in which they passed a great deal of their time. William the Conqueror made a futile attempt to learn English when he was forty-three, (according to Ordericus Vitalis). Henry I may have known a little English. Henry II, the most highly educated sovereign of his day, understood English, but spoke only Latin and French. His son, Richard Coeur de Lion, spent only a few months in England and spoke no English at all. He was thoroughly French, and confined his very considerable poetical talent to that language. Richard's brother, John, well-versed in Latin, it appears, also spoke French. Henry III flooded the country with foreigners, and his sympathies were entirely French, but he probably understood English, and his brother, Richard of Cornwall, who was elected Emperor of Germany, certainly spoke English, a knowledge of which was considered near enough to German to secure his election. Edward I could probably speak some English, and his two successors, Edward II and Edward III, were most likely bi-lingual. Richard II, born in Bordeaux, 1367, son of the Black Prince, spoke fluent English, the order deposing him was read in English, and Henry IV's speeches claiming and accepting the throne were also in English. By the end of the fourteenth century English was firmly established as the language both of law and of literature.

In 1381, Richard of Bordeaux, then a boy of fourteen, faced rebels, 20,000 strong, led by Wat Tyler, Jacke Strawe and John Ball, at Mile End. He boldly addressed them in the vernacular. Later, at Smithfield, when the insolent Wat Tyler had been cut down by the Lord Mayor of London, Richard, quite alone, again courageously confronted large numbers of dangerous insurgents, urging a return to peace and to his authority as king: 'Ye shall have no captain but me. I am your king.' The words, a powerful formula, expertly used, did their work well. Richard made a brave beginning which contrasted sadly with his catastrophic end. 'I write with sorrow of his death,' says Froissart, lamenting the passing of an aesthete, a generous patron of literature, from whose splendid munificence he, amongst other men of letters, had greatly profited.

Richard's successor, Henry IV (Bolingbroke), son of John of Gaunt and Blanche of Lancaster, very different in character and appearance from his aesthetic cousin, was, however, like him, generous to writers, for he continued Chaucer's pension, patronised Gower, and invited Christine de Pisan to England. His will, like those of his son and grandson, was written in English.

Henry V, victor of Agincourt, whose love of learning and of music balanced his brilliant military career, spoke little, we are told, and to the point. He wrote his letters in English, and deserves to be honoured for consciously promoting the use of English, 'procuring the common idiom to be commended by the exercise of writing'. 1422 is a crucial date in the history of the emergence of the vernacular. It was the year in which the Brewers' Craft decided to keep their records in English, following the example of their most excellent lord, the king, whose 'letters missive' were so written. It was at his request that the poet Lydgate translated, from Guido delle Colonne's Latin prose version, the story of the siege of Troy, and to him Occleve dedicated his *De Regimine Principum*. It was in the fifteenth century that English succeeded in displacing both French and Latin in written documents, and great families with commercial interests—Pastons, Celys, Stonors and Plumptons—corresponded freely in English.

The devout founder of Eton, and of King's College, Cambridge, the pious scholar and recluse Henry VI, was, according to his biographer, 'a simple man, without any crook of craft or untruth . . . who would never say an untrue word to any'. Frequent interruptions to his life of devotion in turbulent times merely provoked from him the words, 'They do so interrupt me that by day or night I can hardly snatch a moment to be refreshed by reading of any holy teaching without disturbance.' He spoke English with sober dignity. 'My cousin of York,' he said to his supplanter, Edward of York, 'you are very welcome. I know that in your hands my life will not be in danger.' Three weeks later he was murdered.

The handsome Yorkist Edward IV did not live long to enjoy his restoration, but before he died in 1483 he had proved himself a lavish patron of the arts, spending large sums on manuscript books. Both Hardyng and Capgrave dedicated their works to him. His proficiency in English (he had an English wife) is not in doubt.

The short reign of the last of the Plantagenets, the problematic

Richard III, saw the publication of Malory's *Morte Darthur*, the 'noble and joyous book' which was Caxton's greatest gift to English letters. Before his death on Bosworth Field in 1485, Richard is reported as saying, when defeat was imminent: 'I will not budge a foot.' The terse, defiant words recall an earlier battle and similar sentiments uttered by Englishmen at Maldon in 991.

Henry VII, the first of the Tudors (an upstart dynasty), was of decisively British blood. His mother was Margaret Beaufort, the Lady Margaret who founded two Cambridge colleges and whose name is duly revered today. Her son, thrifty and calculating, brought peace and prosperity to a country disturbed by years of civil strife. At his court art, literature and learning flourished. The poet Skelton was active there, and Erasmus was a visitor. The King, by encouraging Caxton, showed his real concern for letters.

His son, Henry VIII, was an accomplished prince, a fine musician and composer, a good horseman and tennis-player, an excellent linguist, speaking French, Latin, and Spanish. His father perhaps, at one time, intended him for the Archbishopric of Canterbury. His potentialities as a writer were first evinced in his Latin book opposing Luther, the *Assertio Septem Sacramentorum*, which was finished in August, 1521, and translated into English a few years later.

It is in his official English correspondence, his speeches to his parliaments, and his private letters that we can trace the true vigour of his mind, his keen discernment, and his formidable powers of concentration, determination, and pertinacity. He supervised his secretary's work with tremendous care and attention to detail, altering whole passages to make the meaning clearer and to improve the rhythm of the sentences. He had a genuine feeling for the power of words, an impressive grasp of language, and his literary style is always admirably adapted to its purpose.

His love-letters to Anne Boleyn are unexpectedly succinct and businesslike. They waste no time on romantic sentiment or nonsense like that, but express precisely what he has in mind: 'Mine own sweetheart,' he says in one missive, briefly mentioning his yearnings and the headache he has as a result of too much work, 'I wish myself, especially of an evening, in my sweetheart's arms, whose pretty breasts (he uses a more colloquial word) I trust shortly to kiss, written by the hand of him that was, is, and shall be yours by his will, H.R.' Nothing could be more direct. We hear the same brisk and businesslike tone in his addresses to Parliament. I quote from his last speech, December 24th, 1545, in which he, the head of the English Church, shows his concern for his flock:

> I see and hear daily that you of the clergy preach against one another, teach one contrary to another, inveigh one against another without charity or discretion . . . Few or none preach truly and sincerely the word of God, according as they ought to do. Shall I now judge you charitable persons doing this? No, no, I cannot do so. Alas, how can the poor souls live in concord when you preachers sow amongst them in your sermons debate and discord: of you they look for light, and you bring them darkness.

No one could accuse King Henry of drawing out the thread of his verbosity finer than the staple of his argument. These are proper words in proper places—'joined in apt order, that the ear may delight in hearing the harmony'.

His qualities of exceptional intelligence, strong will and the power to convey it in trenchant language he transmitted to his children —Edward VI, Mary, and Elizabeth. The boy king died young, but he was shaping well as a scholar and could express himself clearly both in Latin and in English in a way which reflected credit on his teachers, Richard Cox and Sir John Cheke. In his *Journal* or *Chronicle* for 1551, he described how his Roman Catholic sister, Mary, was summoned before his Council, 'where was declared how long I had suffered her mass, in hope of her reconciliation, and how now being no hope, which I perceived by her letters, except I saw some amendment, I could not bear it. She answered (and the answer is typical of Mary's unswerving attitude) that her soul was God's and her faith she would not change, nor dissemble her opinion with contrary doings. It was said, I constrained not her faith, but wished her, not as a King to rule, but as a subject to obey.' Here is no obscurity but an innate sense of style—the right word in the right place. He was able to report with almost alarming and succinct aloofness the death of his uncle: 'The Duke of Somerset had his head cut off upon Tower-hill, between eight and nine o'clock in the morning.' Had he lived he might have proved as formidable and implacable as his father. His natural brilliance responded well to a careful training in Latin, Greek, and French, and the disciplines of a rigorous education fostered his love of words which he used with skill and daring. He is credited with providing the English language with several new coinages.

The nine-day queen, Lady Jane Grey, was remarkable not only for her courage but also for her phenomenal learning, which was the solace and joy of her short, tragic life, as she confessed to Roger Ascham in impressively plain English, contrasting the 'nips, bobs and pinches' of her severe parents with the gentle enthusiasm of her tutor, Aylmer, later Bishop of London.

Learning graced the Tudor ladies. Mary had no small share of Tudor courage and Tudor eloquence. These were constant characteristics of that family who, in times of danger, could rise to prodigious heights of persuasion. 'Indeed,' says Fuller, speaking of Mary, 'if on just occasion she could not speak confidently and pertinently, she was neither daughter to her father, nor to her mother.' In 1554 she faced up resolutely to the fact of rebellion, and addressed the Londoners at the Guildhall in rousing sentences full of assured courage and confidence in loyalty based on mutual love.

> If a prince and governor may as naturally and earnestly love her subjects as the mother doth love the child, then assure yourselves that I, being your lady and mistress, do as earnestly and tenderly love and favour you. And I, thus loving you, cannot but think that ye as heartily and faithfully love me; and then I doubt not but that we shall give these rebels a short and speedy overthrow . . . Good subjects, pluck up your hearts, and like true men, stand fast against these rebels, both our enemies and yours, and fear them not, for I assure you, I fear them nothing at all.

Such effective eloquence, with its irresistible appeal, through dangers shared, to the hearts of an audience, could not fail to achieve its purpose.

We can recognise the same tones, confident, inspired and appealing, the genuine Tudor note, in the writings and speeches of her learned sister and successor, Elizabeth I. Like her father before her, Elizabeth paid meticulous attention to detail, correcting the drafts of her speeches with tireless concentration and arriving with admirable judgment at the final version. She was a conscious stylist, certain of obtaining the desired effect. In 1566 the question of succession was in the air. From a preliminary draft she developed and delivered to Parliament a brilliant speech, from which I quote:

> Was I not born in the realm? Were my parents born in any foreign country? Is there any cause I should alienate myself from being careful over this country? Is not my kingdom here? Whom have I

oppressed? Whom have I enriched to other's harm? . . . And though I be a woman, yet I have as good a courage, answerable to my place, as ever my father had. I am your anointed Queen. I will never be by violence constrained to do anything. I thank God I am endued with such qualities that if I were turned out of the realm in my petticoat I were able to live in any place in Christendom.

The insistent questions are followed by a short, telling phrase, subtly introducing a reference to her sex which might excuse weakness, but, instead, transcends it.

In 1576 she addressed Parliament in a long oration, replete with wisdom, personal magnetism and a command of literary artifice, which satisfied her critical judgment so well that she had a copy made and sent to her godson, John Harington, then a lad of fourteen or fifteen, bidding him lay it to heart:

Boy Jack, I have made a clerk write fair my poor words for thine use, as it cannot be such striplings have entrance into Parliament assemblies as yet. Ponder them in thy hours of leisure, and play with them till they enter thine understanding. So shalt thou hereafter, perchance, find some good fruits hereof when thy god-mother is out of remembrance.

Here we have her secret—the ability to step off the pedestal, speak simply, and be all things to all men—or boys.

In 1588 the country was in arms against the threat of invasion, and the Queen, having reviewed the troops assembled in London, went to encourage those encamped at Tilbury. With an exact dramatic response to the urgency of the occasion, she harangued her soldiers, in a speech born from a sense of impending danger and courageous indifference to growing menace: 'I know that I have but the body of a weak and feeble woman, but I have the heart of a king, and of a king of England, too . . . Nor will I suffer myself to doubt, but that . . . we shall shortly have a famous victory over those enemies of my God, my kingdom, and my people.' The magnetic appeal was overpowering and the response was total. Later, the great Queen addressed a deputation from the Commons: 'To be a king and wear a crown is a thing more glorious to them that see it than it is pleasant to them that bear it . . . For my own part, . . . it is not my desire to live nor to reign longer than my life and reign shall be for your good. And, though you have had and may have many mightier and wiser princes sitting in this seat, yet you never had nor shall have any love you better.' This is crystal clear. Words and rhythms are those of common speech but used with controlled art to emphasise the sentiment, decorated discreetly according to the idiom of the time. It is perfect epideictic oratory.

Elizabeth's successor, James VI of Scotland and I of England, a Stuart, who could not have been a greater contrast to the Tudors, was, in fact, something of an enigma. Learned he certainly was, for George Buchanan was his tutor, and learning and hunting remained the two passions of his life. Pedantic is too harsh a word to apply to him. He was intolerant of pedantry in others, and, when forced to endure some hours of dull academic speeches, is said to have demanded: 'What do they think I am made of?' He enjoyed theological and political controversy, had a ready wit, together with an argumentative cast of mind. He was the first of our rulers to cherish serious literary aspirations, and his works, enlivened by the play of his intelligence, are easier reading than the ponderous discourses of some of his contemporaries. It is he who is referred to in the Preface to the Authorised Version of the Bible—that wonderful monument of English prose—as its 'Principal Mover and Author'. No mean antagonist—for though sententious, he was shrewd—he was a theorist years in advance of his time. For peace he had a sincere reverence. *Beati Pacifici*, 'Blessed are the peacemakers', was his chosen motto; and garlanded with this device, his unattractive face stares out from the baroque title-page of one of the more lurid Commonwealth accounts of the Jacobean age.

King James, 'God's silly vassal', 'the British Solomon', 'the wisest fool in Christendom', 'Captain of Arts and Clerk of Arms', was a fascinating mixture of contradictions emphasised by the gulf between public sentiment and private behaviour. He had command of two styles, the familiarly colloquial, and the formally ornate, and could be appealing or impressive in both or either. In a period of rapid transition, when religion and politics were closely connected and political ideas could be held to be a branch of ecclesiastical history, it was to be expected that a king of James's education, convictions, and abilities should involve himself with the controversies of his time.

His poetical exercises show less inspiration than ingenuity in interpreting 'reulis and cautelis' (rules and precautions). They are early work and modestly entitled *Essayes of a Prentise in the divine art of Poesie* (1585). His perilous journey from Scotland to Denmark and back, to bring home a queen, so that he might not be 'unjustly slandered as an irresolute ass', as he put it, had an unexpected result. The witches of North Berwick had sought to delay his return with all the miraculous means in their power, and the King presided over their subsequent trials. His interest in the ways of darkness produced the *Daemonologie in forme of a Dialogue*, 1597, typical of the unenlightened attitude of the time.

Among the most interesting of King James's original works is the *Basilicon Doron*, 1599, a book of advice for his son, Henry, Prince of Wales, who died, lamented by the nation, in 1612. James's instructions to his 'dearest son and natural successor' begin with the sonnet:

> God gives not Kings the stile of Gods in vaine,
> For on His throne his scepter doe they sway—

which expresses succinctly his belief in the doctrine of the Divine Right of Kings. This collection of shrewd precepts is couched in a style appropriate to the theme—the education of a young prince —and is clear, precise, and dignified, the effective prose of a man thinking as he writes, and developing his thoughts in a series of short, cumulative clauses:

> First of all things, learn to know and love that God, whom-to you have a double obligation; first, for that he made you a man; and next, for that he made you a little GOD to sit on his throne, and rule over other men . . . Remember to be plaine and sensible in your language; for besides that it is the tongue's office to be the messenger of the mind, it may be thought a point of imbecillitie of spirit in a King, to speak obscurely.

From excellent advice on speech, the King turns to instruction on written works: 'Now as to your writing, *which is nothing else but a form of enregistrate speech*; use a plaine, short, but stately stile . . . And I would also advise you to *write in your own language*: for there is nothing left to be said in Greeke and Latine.' We should remember James's saying, 'If I were not a King I would be a University man.' He might have made a worthy don.

His formal speeches, delivered with a strong Scottish accent, display his studied eloquence. In his first address to the Upper House in March, 1603, he declared: '. . . that his tongue should be ever the trew Messenger of his heart'. In March, 1607 the King's speech before both Houses culminated in an excellent example of the type of eloquence he delighted in: 'I will not say anything which I will not promise, nor promise anything which I will not swear; what I will swear I will sign, and what I sign I shall with God's grace ever perform.' The meaning is unmistakable and arrived at by a series of well-defined steps, leading to a conclusive climax.

In 1609 he considered the problem of the Common Law, anticipating remarkably the Act of 1650, that Law Reports should be in the vernacular.

A Counterblaste to Tobacco appeared anonymously in 1604. In this tract King James inveighs with a vigorous diatribe, as apposite now as then, against the habit of smoking:

> Surely smoke becomes a kitchen far better than a Dining chamber, and yet it makes a kitchen also oftentimes in the inward parts of men, soiling and infecting them, with an unctuous and oily kinde of soote, as hath bene found in some great Tobacco takers, that after their death were opened . . .

The conclusion crashes into a resounding climax:

> Have you not reason then to be ashamed, and to forbeare this filthie noveltie, so basely grounded, so foolishly received and so grossely mistaken in the right use thereof? . . . A custome lothsome to the eye, hatefull to the Nose, harmefull to the braine, dangerous to the Lungs, and in the blacke stinking fume thereof, neerest resembling the horrible Stigian smoke of the pit that is bottomelesse.

We cannot escape the conclusion that, in his formal writings, Parliamentary speeches, controversial treatises, and familiar letters —those to 'Baby Charles', and to his 'sweet child and wife', his 'sweetheart', his 'sweet Steenie', George Villiers, whose picture he wore next his heart and upon whose heart-roots he invoked 'blessings, blessings, blessings', in a torrent of unrestrained emotion, we have a speech-based prose, strong, flexible, eloquent and memorable—a prose for all seasons, which all educated men of sense and feeling could manipulate with skill and employ effectively. We might remember that, to use his own words, King James considered writing 'but a form of enregistrate speech'.

King James's successors did not share his serious literary aspirations but they used the vernacular with confident ability and an innate sense of style, if by style we can assume the clearest expression of meaning in the fewest possible words. They were all, to some extent, victims of a turbulent age of unrest, and in the cases of Charles I and James II were prepared to sacrifice throne for convictions. It is not for me now to comment on the memorable scene of Charles I's martyrdom, but to express admiration for his powerful use of words in all situations, melancholy, happily domestic, pleasantly affectionate, controversial or political. His son, the second Charles, brave, most brilliantly gifted, a man.

so various that he seemed to be/Not one, but all mankind's epitome,

charming, witty, cynical, fascinating, kind, philosophic, reputed to be the best conversationalist of the age, was a master of the telling phrase. 'My words are my own but my acts are my ministers',' was his ready reply to the derisory sneer,

He never said a foolish thing/And never did a wise one.

His speeches, and his correspondence, formal or personal, reveal his masterly use of the vernacular to express the wide range of his interests, from sentimental (the delightful letters to his beloved sister, his 'dearest Minette') to artistic, political and scientific. Everyone knows about the mischievous question he posed at a meeting of the Royal Society: 'Why does a living fish weigh more than a dead one?' interrupting the disputants to enquire whether any of them had begun by verifying the assumed fact.

His brother James II lacked his 'charisma', but, like his father, was ready to sacrifice throne for convictions. Unfortunate, like most of his line, he wrote in exile from England the *Memoirs* of his life. The diarists Pepys and Evelyn both refer to him with appreciation.

Of his two daughters by Anne Hyde, his first wife, it is not necessary to speak at length. Mary, the elder, who became the consort of William III, was the more intelligent and able. The education of both ladies had suffered from the times and was almost purely domestic. Anne, at loggerheads with her sister and brother-in-law (she dubbed them 'the Calibans'), was hampered by ill-health, and many pregnancies. She is said to have lacked originality, but there are signs of it in her personal correspondence and its world of fantasy. In this she was fluent enough, addressing her dear friend Sarah Churchill, Duchess of Marlborough, as Mrs Freeman and signing herself as Mrs Morley. There is no eloquence here, but the playful language of escape from an uncomfortable real world.

From first to last the male Stuarts had the art of arousing devotion

—well-intentioned, misunderstood, proud, obstinate and courageous, they shared a care for literature, for art, and for music, together with a skill in the use of words, which, transmitted across the centuries, survived to distinguish some of their successors.

As you know, the immediate successors to the Stuarts were Hanoverians. They were direct descendants of Sophia, daughter of Elizabeth, Queen of Bohemia, and grand-daughter of James I. She was married to Ernst Augustus, Duke of Hanover. Her son, George I, spoke no English and for him Hanover remained the centre of his universe. His son, George II, was taught English, together with French and Latin, and spoke the tongue of his adopted country with a strong German accent. 'I hate all Boets and Bainters,' he was alleged to have declared on one occasion. When his dying wife urged him to marry again he blurted out, 'Non, non, j'aurai des maîtresses.' A choleric little man, kicking his wig round the room in a rage, he was a brave soldier, and at Dettingen he placed himself at the head of his troops. This Hanoverian combined Teutonic bellicosity with British phlegm. With complete composure he received the news of the Young Pretender's presence at Derby in 1745. Calm in the midst of panic, he was alleged to have made, with enviable sang-froid, a typically terse remark: 'Pooh! Don't talk to me dat stoff!' and to have gone on eating his Schweinskopf and Sauerkraut.

George III, the son of Frederick, Prince of Wales, 'Poor Fred, who was alive and is dead. There is no more to be said', was far from being the nonentity you might have expected from such a father. But he had a formidable mother. 'George, be a King!' she used to exhort him. George persevered and developed into a model father and beneficent sovereign whose domestic bliss and views on literature have been carefully recorded by Fanny Burney. He spoke French, German, Italian, and Latin as well as English. 'Born and educated in this country, I glory in the name of Briton,' he inserted in his own writing into his accession speech. Nothing could have endeared him more to his people. The books which he collected with zeal and veneration still remain in the British Library.

As she presents them to us, the Royals, to use Miss Burney's term, appear simple, generous-hearted people, fond of each other, leading quiet lives with dignity and complacency. 'Nobody answered,' says the author of *Evelina*, when the King announced, 'I think him a monster. I own it fairly.' He was talking of Voltaire. Encouraged by lack of comment he went on to Rousseau, 'charging him with savage pride and insolent ingratitude', but was becomingly silenced by Miss Burney's recalling that her father had noticed a portrait of the King over the chimney when he had visited Rousseau in his garret. Mrs Siddons impressed the monarch: 'I am an enthusiast for her, quite an enthusiast. I think there was never any player in my time so excellent —not Garrick himself. I own it!'

Finally he came to Shakespeare: 'Was there ever such stuff as the great part of Shakespeare? Only one must not say so! But what think you? What? Is there not sad stuff? What? What?' Miss Burney's reply to this frank outburst was a model of tact: 'Yes, indeed, I think so, Sir, though mixed with such excellences that . . .' 'Oh!' cried the King. 'I know it is not to be said! But it's true. Only it's Shakespeare, and nobody dare abuse him!' What more could we expect from such a kindly, charitable, sociable, and ordinary potentate as 'Farmer George'?

The fourth King George deserves to be particularly remembered here as the first very generous patron of this Royal Society of Literature, founded in 1823.

The Stuarts' charm evaded most of the Hanoverians, but fortunately for us remained to adorn with its magic the image of Queen Victoria. Had she not been a queen, Victoria would have excelled as a journalist and perhaps as a royal Barbara Cartland. She had a natural talent for writing, and was a highly successful, compulsive diarist. She possessed an excellent, retentive memory, together with keen observation, and her vehement, intense, sincere feelings, poured out at full speed, were expressed with vivid exactitude. She spoke German till she was three, learned English with ease, and spoke it in a clear voice with beautiful precision. Mother of nine children, she found time amidst the cares of family and State to write her *Leaves from a Journal of Our Life in the Highlands, 1848–61*, published privately 1867, publicly 1868, with a second part, *More Leaves*, (1862–82), 1883. Every day she corresponded with her daughter the Empress of Germany, and composed her diary. There were 122 volumes of that, but, alas, it was mostly destroyed by her daughter, Princess Beatrice, her literary executor.

Leaves was dedicated 'to the memory of him who made the life of the writer bright and happy' and like its sequel is suffused with a deep and tender melancholy. *More Leaves* invoked the memory of her 'devoted personal attendant and faithful friend John Brown' and both books share the intimacy of a family journal with simple, clear descriptions of impressive scenery and visits to dignified peasantry. 'I went,' wrote the Queen,

> into a small cabin of old Kitty Kears, who is 86 years old—quite erect and who welcomed us with a great air of dignity. She sat down and spun. I gave her . . . a warm petticoat; she said, 'May the Lord ever attend ye and yours, here and hereafter; and may the Lord be a guide to ye, and keep ye from all harm.'

Victoria's interest in and genuine pity for the poor are obvious, but mixed with admiration for their quiet acceptance of their hard lot. Scotland, 'beloved Scotland', is pronounced the 'proudest, finest country in the world', 'where there was such devoted loyalty to the family of my ancestors, for Stuart blood is in my veins, and I am *now* their representative and the people are as devoted and loyal to me as they were to that unhappy race'. She exclaims 'What a scene it must have been in 1745! And here was I, the descendant of the Stuarts and of the very king whom Prince Charles sought to overthrow, sitting and walking about quite privately and peaceably.' The simplicity of her language aptly conveys her feelings of reverence for 'that most beautiful country' which she was proud to call her own.

With keen perception and typical shrewdness, Queen Victoria recognised her chief quality. Writing to her daughter, then Crown Princess of Prussia, she said: 'If old Mama has a merit it is that of truth and the absence of all flattery and a tolerably quick and correct appreciation of character,' and she was right. Intense, emotional, affectionate and obstinate she might have been, but she was always honest, always sincere. She wrote as she spoke, with vigour, clarity and common-sense, and easily found the appropriate words and style to suit the circumstances. She could be massively impressive. She could be wryly humorous, referring to the frequency of royal births as reminding her of the ways of the rabbits in Windsor Park. If constantly aware of the responsibilities of her position, she was deeply aware also of the dangers of discrimination against race or class. In December 1867, she wrote: 'The lower classes are becoming so well-informed, are so intelligent and earn their bread and riches so deservedly—that they cannot and ought not to be kept back—to be abused by the wretched, ignorant, high-born beings who live only to kill time.' And in August 1868: 'I do feel so strongly that we are before God all alike, and that in the twinkling of an eye, the highest may find themselves at the feet of the poorest and lowest. I have seen the noblest, most refined, high-bred feelings in the humblest and most unlearned, and this it is most necessary a Prince should feel.' It was her conviction that 'division of classes is the *one thing* which is most dangerous and reprehensible, never intended by the law of nature', and she rammed home the thought with the words, 'the Archbishop of York's father was a butcher and *so on*'.

She shared with the writers of the age an astounding vitality—great energy, producing sometimes an embarrassing wealth of words—and an enviable mastery of fluent expression.

Her descendants have become increasingly aware of the great potentiality of English. It is the reigning monarch who broadcasts a Christmas message every year, following a tradition started by King George V, continued by his son King George VI, and carried on by Queen Elizabeth II, patron of this Royal Society of Literature—in English, in simple, sincere, impressive and memorable language. In his address to the English Association, of which he was then President, His Royal Highness Prince Philip expressed his interest in language, especially in language as a means of communication, concluding weightily that 'the ability to communicate intelligently is the single most important factor in the future progress—indeed survival —of human civilisation'. It is in this area of achievement that English is conspicuously successful.

I have tried to show that some of our kings and queens have employed our common vernacular with splendid authority. By their ability to use their language well, they have helped to promote and establish its wide currency, and to maintain the global supremacy of English in all its manifestations—in fact, to justify the superiority suggested by the title ROYAL ENGLISH.

THE CHILDREN'S WRITER: ARTIST OR TEACHER'S AID

GEOFFREY TREASE FRSL

Read 13th May 1982:
Nina Bawden, JP, FRSL, in the Chair

I NEVER knew Joseph Bard, whose memory we honour today. But all I have heard of his lively mind and wide cultural interests encourages me to think he would not have been unsympathetic to my choice of subject. He wrote little himself, he was certainly not a children's writer, but in one of his few works, *The Tale of a Child*, set in his native Hungary in 1900, he used an eight-year-old narrator, his own age at that date. So clearly he recognised and respected the distinctive vision of the young.

I hope that my title will not be misconstrued in any sense of hostility to my many good friends in the world of education. Even the hungriest author would be short-sighted indeed if he bit the hand that fed him. Most children's writers are only too grateful for the stimulus and encouragement (not to mention the material benefits) they derive from the use of their work in schools.

The partnership of storyteller and schoolmaster is as old as classical Greece, where the *Iliad* was a corner-stone of education. We have no evidence that this caused Homer to turn in his grave, though we might welcome the biographical evidence such soil disturbance would provide. Homer might rather have been gratified, like later authors, to know that his tales were read in school. He might even have accepted, as we do, the somewhat ambiguous distinction of having passages set as comprehension tests. One is never quite sure whether this is an accolade or a veiled criticism. He might have submitted to those letters from pupils set to carry out projects on their 'favourite author'. I received one myself from a schoolgirl propounding fourteen numbered questions, of which No. 6 was 'How did you meet your wife?' What would we not give, today, for such a fan-letter from Xenophon to Homer—and the poet's reply?

As it is, we must assume that Homer was not a children's author, and composed his stories untroubled by any thought of their future academic utility. No one indeed, for ages, considered children as a special audience. In England the first book for them came in 1477, when Caxton produced *The Book of Courtesy*. It sounded at once the didactic note that was to dominate juvenile publications for centuries. It was no swashbuckling adventure yarn but a guide to behaviour, full of such unexciting admonitions as 'Do not dip your thumb in your drink, because it is not courteous.' Only much later came the revolutionary notion that a child's book might include a modest element of entertainment.

The pioneer was that enterprising printer, publisher and purveyor of quack medicines, John Newbery. His *Little Pretty Pocket Book*, in 1744, had pictures and poems 'intended for the Instruction and Amusement of Little Master Tommy and Pretty Miss Polly'—and a preface 'humbly addressed to all Parents, Guardians, Governesses, etc, wherein Rules are laid down for making their Children strong, healthy, virtuous, wise and happy.' Seventeen years later Newbery ventured on his first original storybook, which some think he commissioned from his friend Goldsmith. *Goody Two-shoes* is usually regarded as the foundation-stone of juvenile fiction. But of course children had long enjoyed the old tales retold for them in chapbooks. Boswell's *London Journal* has an entry dated 10 July, 1763:

> . . . some days ago I went to the old printing-office in Bow Churchyard kept by Dicey, whose family have kept it fourscore years. There are ushered into the world of literature *Jack and the Giants*, *The Seven Wise Men of Gotham*, and other story-books which in my dawning years amused me as much as *Rasselas* does now. I saw the whole scheme with a kind of pleasing romantic feeling to find myself really where all my old darlings were printed.

He bought two dozen and had them bound up. The volume is now in the library at Harvard, with his own inscription:

I shall certainly some time or other write a little story-book in the style of these. It will not be a very easy task for me; it will require much nature and simplicity and a great acquaintance with the humours and traditions of the English common people. I shall be happy to succeed, for he who pleases children will be remembered with pleasure by men.

Like many of Boswell's resolutions this was never kept. One would have given much to see what that eminent moralist would have done in the field of junior fiction. Clearly the idea was in the air now, that new books might be written for the entertainment, not just the improvement, of the young.

The idea caught on, but not without opposition. Sarah Trimmer gave warning: 'There is not a species of Books for Children and Youth which has not been made in some way or other an engine of mischief.' In her own *Fabulous Histories* she was torn between the demands of factual accuracy and moral uplift. Morality won. One of her footnotes is remembered when the rest of her book is forgotten: 'A mockbird is properly a native of America, but is introduced here for the sake of the moral.' By 1821 the menace of children's fiction had assumed for some the horrific implications now associated with television. Maria Hack doubted 'whether habituating children to seek amusement, almost exclusively, in fictitious narrative, has not a direct tendency to weaken the natural powers.'

Even the old stories fell under suspicion. *Cinderella* was accused of depicting 'some of the worst passions that can enter into the human breast—envy, jealousy, vanity, a love of dress.' One writer corrected these faults by turning the story into temperance propaganda. Cinderella's marriage to Prince Charming was celebrated with a bonfire on to which every cask of wine from the palace cellars was exultantly thrown. Some may question nowadays whether readers of a tender age should be exposed to scenes of such horror.

The emphasis continued to be on uplift rather than information. Facts, after all, could be inculcated by the memorising of lists or that favourite teacher's stand-by, Mangnall's Questions. This volume, *Historical and Miscellaneous Questions for the Use of Young People*, was compiled by a Wakefield schoolmistress, Richmal Mangnall. It came out in 1800 and had a long vogue—my mother used to tell me how she was subjected to it as a schoolgirl in the eighteen-eighties. Some people did realise, however, that an entertaining story could also convey information. One such survives in *The Swiss Family Robinson*. Most of us, at some time, have wandered in fancy over that extraordinary island with its improbably varied flora and fauna—compared with which even Kew Gardens combined with the Zoo might seem a shade monotonous. This absurd but vastly entertaining tale was the creation of a Swiss pastor, Johann David Wyss, for the edification of his sons. Many years later one of them touched up his manuscript and published it in 1812. William Godwin seized upon it with enthusiasm for his Juvenile Library series and was busy translating it from the German just when Shelley was planning to elope with Mary—it has been said, indeed, that Shelley gave his future father-in-law some help with the translation. Lovers will sometimes undertake the most incongruous tasks to further their designs. Godwin's edition came out with the sub-title, 'a Practical Illustration of the First Principles of Mechanics, Natural Philosophy, Natural History, and all those branches of Science which most immediately apply to the business of Life.' Teacher's aid indeed.

It has been claimed that not until *Alice in Wonderland*, in 1865, did children get a story of pure entertainment without the least trace element of educational value. Within the last month even this claim has been questioned. I see from the *Times* Diary an assurance by a vice-president of the British Computer Society, that 'computer people read *Alice* to enhance their conceptual understanding of programming languages.' But at least, before 1865, the old kind of explicit instruction was giving place to something subtler. The adventure-story had arrived, and its boy heroes were used to personify the values of the Victorian middle class. Accuracy was aimed at, especially in history and geography, but it was incidental to the action.

Ballantyne's *Coral Island* was a far cry from the Swiss Family Robinson. Ballantyne had begun by writing from his first-hand experience with the Hudson's Bay Company, but he knew little of the Pacific. He had seen coconuts on fair-grounds, but he was mortified to learn too late, after publication, about the thick outer husk they wear on coral islands. In all his subsequent stories he went to great lengths to acquire direct experience.

Henty, though, was the man for eyewitness accuracy. As a war correspondent he had stood on the battlefields of the Crimea, been out with Garibaldi, been through the Franco-Prussian and the Balkan wars, and marched upcountry in West Africa and Abyssinia. Despite all the carnage he saw, he never lost his love of military glory. Even Henty had sometimes to write from secondhand experience. He had been born too late to ride an elephant with Hannibal. So for his earlier periods his method was to send to the London Library for half a dozen reliable history-books and out of them spin his yarn—lying back on his sofa, pipe in hand, dictating to a male secretary, six or seven thousand words a day. He was not concerned with psychological niceties in foreigners and former centuries: it has been complained that all his heroes were Victorian school prefects, costumed for their parts.

Schoolmasters not surprisingly approved of Henty. He wrote good English—which meant that it was grammatical if not inspired. It was 'healthy stuff', any amount of slaughter but no goings-on with the opposite sex. In his last book, *With the Allies to Pekin*, he describes with gusto how two fearless lads encounter a dozen homicidal Orientals, and are able, thanks to their magazine-loading rifles, to wipe them out in a few moments. But Henty once told an interviewer: 'No, I never touch a love interest. Once I ventured to make a boy of twelve kiss a little girl of eleven, and I received a very indignant letter from a dissenting minister.'

Victorian authors had to watch their step, but they could survive occasional disapproval from individuals because they were meeting an immense demand. They did not depend on schools and public libraries: they sold to a prosperous middle class which, in those dear dead days beyond recall, *bought* books. It is said that on the morning when a new Ballantyne came out, the street outside his publisher's office was jammed with fashionable carriages. So the approval of schoolmasters, though not unwelcome, did not dominate. They might buy occasional stories by living authors to hand out on the platform as prizes—it is not so long since publishers still used the heading in catalogues, 'Rewards and Prizes'—but few nineteenth-century teachers would have taken contemporary fiction into their classrooms. For serious education they felt much as the old-time Indian fighter felt: the only good author, like the only good Injun, was a dead one. Even now that idea lingers with a strange obstinacy in children's minds, though few teachers hold it themselves. How uncomfortably often have I heard of its being applied to my own name. 'What? Is he still alive?' The question would hardly have arisen a century ago. The contemporary storyteller did not rub shoulders confusingly with the

classics. He was nothing to do with education. He was an entertainer.
If good enough he was, like other imaginative writers, a literary
artist.

Literature is a word of wide meanings, extending even to the glossy
holiday brochures that flop through our letterboxes. I use it here in the
generally understood sense implicit in the name of this society
—something committed to paper that is worth saying and is expressed
with a certain artistic skill.

In that sense, I submit, children's books by the end of the
nineteenth century had long escaped from their didactic beginnings.
They deserved to be regarded as literature—a junior branch, perhaps,
but an integral and not unbeautiful or unfruitful part of the whole
tree. The thirty years starting with *Masterman Ready* in 1841 had
produced works as varied as Lear's *Book of Nonsense* and Ruskin's
King of the Golden River, *Tom Brown's Schooldays*, *Alice* and *Little
Women*. In one period of about twelve months came *The Rose and the
Ring*, *The Lances of Lynwood*, *The Young Fur Traders*, and *Westward
Ho!* If the best of these do not amount to literature, should we not alter
our definition?

Yet in the histories of English literature where are they? I take down
from my own bookshelf the thick volume of Legouis and Cazamian.
In nearly 1400 pages they cover English literature from the year 635 to
1940. I scan their index—thirty-four small-print columns. It is very
learned, very comprehensive. Too grand, of course, for Henty or
Ballantyne. Yet it is equally silent about Lear and Lewis Carroll. For a
moment my heart leaps up as I see 'Hughes, Thomas'. But no, on
looking him up, I find he is not the immortal creator of Tom
Brown—he is an obscure Elizabethan playwright who wrote *The
Misfortunes of Arthur*, acted at Gray's Inn in 1588, and, I imagine, not
very often since.

The few children's writers who slip into this magisterial survey are
those who cannot be excluded, because they wrote also for an adult
public. Cazamian cannot ignore Stevenson. And, having mentioned
him, he cannot ignore *Treasure Island*, because, boys' story or not, it is
one of the chief books for which Stevenson is remembered. And once
he has admitted its existence, Cazamian's enthusiasm knows no
bounds. He commends 'the craft of the story-teller, the intensity of
the episodes, the vividness of the exotic scenes and of the main
characters'. But, he continues, 'they grow out of a more profound
intuition—that of the imaginative appeal, of the dramatic progress,

and the moral originality of the themes; and this is an intuition of a psychological order.'

If this is not the very stuff of literature, what is? The characterisation of Long John Silver, he says, is 'worthy of a great artist'. Yet one wonders if *Treasure Island* would have found its honoured niche in this literary history if Stevenson had not also written for adults. What if he had written a dozen superb adventure-stories, but had never travelled with a donkey or made an inland voyage?

This attitude seems general, if not universal, in this field of studies. It comes from no ill-will. There is no concerted policy to regard the children's authors as the lepers of literature. I suspect that they are excluded because no one can see quite where to fit them in.

Scholars have an urge to classify. They may departmentalise literature according to its form—the novel, the drama, lyric poetry, and so on. Or by period—Elizabethan, Restoration, Augustan. Or by language and territory—Spanish or German, American or Australian. They are not accustomed to consider the age of the intended audience. So they are puzzled when faced, say, with a junior novel—a piece of fiction addressed primarily to the young adolescent, though often enjoyed by much older people. Nowadays such a book may not be blood-and-thunder—it is likely to be a perceptive study of human relationships. Yet it cannot be lumped in with the works of Angus Wilson and Iris Murdoch—any more than those delightful children's plays by the late Nicholas Stuart Gray can be considered along with the dramas of Christopher Fry, let alone those of Osborne or Beckett. Publishers in their lists, booksellers and librarians in their shops and libraries, are driven to an arbitrary segregation—but at least it is usually only a few short steps to pass from one set of shelves to another, and it is not a one-way traffic—just as the growing child makes sorties to the adult department, so many an adult unashamedly finds pleasure, not only, like Boswell, in re-reading an old darling, but in discovering, sometimes with incredulous delight, the remarkably different kind of book being published for young people today. It is the words that matter, not the numbers in the library catalogue. We recognise genuine literature, whatever shelf we take it from, as Housman recognised poetry. For myself I believe that the best writing for children *is* literature and that its authors *should* be assessed primarily as literary artists, not as educational auxiliaries, with dinner-ladies and Lollipop men. Where the academics of the English Department are to fit them in I must leave them to decide.

If they can do it only by establishing a Children's Corner I suppose that misleading label must be accepted with good humour. But a *place* in literature they do deserve.

Some may object, feelings are all very well—the shiver down the spine, the sensation in the pit of the stomach, by which Housman recognised poetry—but we should prefer to be persuaded on more intellectual grounds. *Is* this cold-shouldering of children's books just a tiresome little problem of classification? Or has even the finest children's book a fatal disqualifying deficiency because it is addressed to an immature public?

I know that when I write what my publisher will classify as a 'children's' book I must ignore the many older people who will read it. I must aim at the centre of the target—let us say children between ten and fourteen—though I know it is a target with many outer rings, ranging from eight to eighty. G. M. Trevelyan told me, towards the end of his life, how much he was enjoying historical adventure-stories. But octogenarians must not enter into one's calculations. The target is childhood and early adolescence. I am not sure which is the more odious, the old-fashioned 'talking down', the unmistakable tone of condescension, or the conspiratorial wink directed at one's fellow-adults. I say to myself, some of these children are certainly more intelligent than I am, some have specialised knowledge I do not possess, some have an intuition and understanding that would humble me, were I to meet them face to face. I can make *no* assumptions about them as individuals—except that I have lived longer, and collected much more clutter of background information in general, and can pick up references and elliptical allusions that might puzzle them.

But when was lack of sophistication a bar to the appreciation of literature? Primitive peoples evolve folk-tales and poems of high quality. Homer's first audiences were unsophisticated, even the classical Athenian was an ignoramus compared with a twelve-year-old today. We must not, of course, confuse knowledge and sophistication with maturity, but it is just as mistaken to suppose that maturity is only biological and that young readers cannot enter imaginatively into fields of human experience that, in their own lives, can only lie ahead. We acknowledge the wonderful capacity for empathy in countless novelists—our adult literature is full of vicarious experience, brilliantly evoked—and if that imaginative leap is possible for so many writers, surely a much less demanding effort must be within the power of the readers.

In which case, it may be argued, what need for a separate juvenile literature? Why should not children wander at will among the adult shelves, taking down whatever they are ready to absorb? They should, of course. And do. Some of them. But it is not quite so simple as that. Apart from practical questions, such as format and length, there is the matter of identification, of point of view. A child can comprehend a great deal of human experience, even old age and death, but it can do so most easily through the eyes of its own age-group. As indeed Stevenson understood, when he made Jim Hawkins, the cabin-boy, the narrator of *Treasure Island*. There have, of course, been many good children's books without a youthful character at their centre, but this instinct to identify is very powerful. And it becomes increasingly important for understanding when we move away from romantic adventure into the realms of everyday emotion and experience.

Those of us whose own childhood is distant do not always realise what a revolution has occurred in the subject-matter now open to the writer for the young.

When I began work almost fifty years ago juvenile literature was at its lowest ebb. Henty had died in 1902, but his shadow lay heavily across the adventure-story. The Great War had produced a convulsion in every area of adult literature, but in children's fiction the values of Henty stood firm. War was still glorious. One Englishman still equalled two Frenchmen, four Germans, and a proportionally larger number of other aliens. Natives were loyal if they supported their colonial masters, treacherous if not. An aristocratic bias was normal, and the common people figured mainly as simple peasants, faithful retainers, or howling mob. Girls were reluctantly admitted to the excitement, as second-class boys, if they had the stamina not to slow down the action. No wonder that George Orwell was complaining, as late as 1940, that boys' fiction was sodden in the worst illusions of 1910.

It was an age of hackwork. Reputable publishers expected to buy outright copyright for fifty pounds, and there was little inducement to writers of talent to enter the field. Leaving aside those with reputations elsewhere, who could not be got on such terms—Kipling and Milne, Masefield and de la Mare—only a few first-class talents emerged among authors thought of primarily, or solely, as writing for children. A manual published in 1929, *Writing for Children*, offered formulae for success. Beginners wishing to emulate Talbot Baines Reed or Angela Brazil were given this advice:

With regard to ideas the best method of obtaining them is to put into words those beautiful day-dreams of one's youth. To bring off that marvellous catch; to rescue the headmaster's little daughter from the mill-stream; to stumble across the cache of silver articles stolen from the home of the School governor; to win the 'Mile' with one's arm hanging at one's side after the School bully has fouled one on the bend; to struggle against the swift current in the river with the youngest girl in the school clinging round one's neck; and to save one's favourite mistress from financial disaster. Make the characters live the lives of ordinary healthy human boys or girls.

Such formulae at best produced a good deal of harmless entertainment. Sometimes, possibly, they produced attitudes of mind we may now deplore. Certainly they did not produce books of originality or quality, and it has been the lingering memory of people nourished on such stories in their youth that has made it hard for them, later, to consider children's books seriously.

Change was coming. By 1940 a distinguished new American writer, James Daugherty, was pouring scorn on 'the complacent oldsters satisfied with handing the rising generation a gas-mask and a copy of *Alice in Wonderland* with which to tread the bomb-strewn path of childhood.' Children's literature, he argued, was devitalised when writers refused to look the present in the face, and enriched when writers confronted, and made their readers confront, the problems and paradoxes of their own time.

By 1946 a New Zealand librarian, Dorothy Neal White, could say:

Children's literature has . . . broadened its range and increased in depth . . . Children's literature has been slowly maturing, as modern knowledge—political science, sociology, anthropology, economics—all impinged upon it. Some men and women will regret that children's literature is becoming more and more concerned with the facts of life, in both a political and biological sense, and there may be some cause for melancholy whenever the sweet swift dream of childhood is disturbed. I think, however, that children's literature has gained rather than lost by its new awareness of the world and the way it works.

Mrs White's study, *About Books for Children*, was—significantly —published by the New Zealand Council for Educational Research. The educationists were already starting to annex the territory ignored by the students of literature. An honoured flag, but not the one to which the imaginative writer owes his first allegiance.

The tendencies Mrs White noticed were then perhaps more evident in America, but they quickly gained ground here in the nineteen-fifties. Some of the old taboos died hard. I too, like Henty, incurred the rebuke of Nonconformity. I had described two adult characters and four adolescents consuming a bottle of Sauterne at Christmas. The editor of a religious weekly asked me if I thought it right 'to introduce young children to the cocktail habit'. And the editor of *John o' London's*, that much-loved Yorkshireman, Wilson Midgley, told me that he had enjoyed my story, but why did I 'spoil it on the last page by hinting that the boy was getting fond of the girl?'

I dare not think what he would have said about the books being published twenty years later. I recall seeing a delightful and straight-forward picture-book for seven-year-olds, which explained conception and pregnancy. It was engagingly entitled *Inside Mum*. But what would really have shaken Midgley would have been the spate of outspoken junior novels. I saw some of the themes listed in a specialist review: 'a series of promiscuous affairs, backstreet abortion, adolescent homosexuality . . .' I quote without enthusiasm—the actual volumes never came my way—but the list indicates that few aspects of life are now excluded.

Not every storyteller wishes to explore such controversial areas. Not every storyteller wants to say anything to the child at all, and some indignantly repudiate the notion—the early emphasis on moralising and didacticism has so long been ridiculed, and in reaction many feel that entertainment should be the sole objective. I wonder. We are accustomed to ask, about writers for adults, 'Yes, fine, but has he anything to *say*? May not the question be legitimately asked of a children's author? An optional question, but not irrelevant. Many do wish to make a statement and it has not diminished their popularity. To quote Diana Wynne Jones: 'I try to use fantasy—just as one would use a metaphor—to says things about life. It seems to me that very complicated things can be said to children by these simple means . . . Each time I write a book I try to say something new.' And the Australian Patricia Wrightson puts it bluntly: 'It occurred to me that if I, as a mother, had nothing worth saying to children, the outlook for my own children was pretty poor.'

The communication need not be explicitly conveyed. Children may be of the same age-group and at the same stage in arithmetic, but not at the same point of readiness to comprehend the world widening in front of them. The wise storyteller will not force information down unwilling throats, but it will be there, implicit in his text, for those able to absorb it. Another fantasy-writer, Alan Garner, puts it well:

> In order to connect, the book must be written for all levels of experience . . . any given piece of text must work at simple plot level, so that the reader feels compelled to turn the page, if only to find out what happens next; but it must also work for me, and for every stage between. My concern for the reader is not to bore him. Anything else that comes through in the book is pure bonus. An onion can be peeled down through its layers, but it is always, at every layer, an onion, whole in itself. I try to write onions.

I too try to write onions. Alan Garner's approach is in essence the one I have long used myself. It can be applied to many types of book. Biography for young readers is one example. Here one has to handle themes that would once have been barred as wildly unsuitable. My American publisher once asked me for a short life of Byron for boys and girls who would meet his poetry at school but would know little of the man, his story and his period. The idea excited me. But when I discussed it with one of my British publishers—this was 1968—the reaction was nervous. All that business about Augusta. And Clare Clairmont. And, oh dear, so many other scandals, without which Byron would not have been Byron, and without which the book would have been very short indeed. Another of my publishers agreed to my proposal, but with heavy misgivings. I wrote the book. It was an onion, strongly flavoured as onions tend to be, potentially indigestible. But in fact there was not a hiccup of complaint.

I followed it with a junior biography of D. H. Lawrence. Both books could be peeled down through their layers, to suit the comprehension of readers at varying stages of maturity. Both men had obligingly led lives that, in Garner's phrase, 'worked at simple plot level'. Byron's was fuller of more obviously extravagant adventure, but Lawrence's was hardly devoid of incident. There was the elopement with the extraordinary Frieda, the farcical incongruity of Lawrence's being thought a British spy in Germany and a German spy in England—and the police raid on his picture-exhibition, their suspicions enhanced when they found there a book in French—actually a translation of *The Hunting of the Snark*—suspicions in no way diminished when they were told that the author had been a clergyman. There was plenty to hold quite a young reader's interest. And, that assured, one could include the deeper layers, and maturer adolescents would absorb as much as they were ready for.

Kipling used the method before any of us. He was looking back on *Rewards and Fairies*, a quarter of a century after he wrote it. He said: 'I worked the material in three or four overlaid tints and textures, which might or might not reveal themselves according to the shifting light of sex, youth and experience.' And can we say that Kipling, when writing his children's books, was any less an artist than in his other work?

So, the children's writer is not limited in his subject-matter. Let us turn to the other vital question, is he so limited in language that his work cannot be taken seriously by artistic standards? We may think that question sufficiently answered by the mere naming of Kipling, and Stevenson, Oscar Wilde and Mark Twain. But, as we have seen, such authors are accorded respect because of their fame in other fields. Yet superb children's books have been written by other people who wrote nothing else—or by people like E. Nesbit, whose copious output of adult fiction, poetry and plays, is now almost forgotten. It is these writers, who stand or fall by the quality of their children's books, who may still have to establish their claim to be first-class citizens in the republic of letters.

The linguistic limitation has been much exaggerated. Anatole France advises us, 'When you are writing for children, do not assume a style for the occasion. Think your best and write your best.' Roy Fuller has said, 'Though writing for children has always given me a certain sense of freedom, I have never thought of my children's books as "written down" to an audience.' Some of us write with declared disregard of our readers' ages. Others—you and I, Madam Chairman, I believe, among them—admit to making some conscious adjustment. It need not be a big one. Rosemary Sutcliff says, 'The difference between writing for children and for adults is, to me at any rate, only a quite small gear-change.' That is well put. The 'small gear-change' in my own case means striving more than ever for clarity—not necessarily always for simplicity, but rather for the concrete instead of the abstract, as I was taught to do at school when writing Greek and Latin prose. Not that simplicity too, as Bunyan demonstrated, ever hindered any one from writing magnificently.

Surely, some one will say, children are unconscious of style?

Perhaps. But good writing is not wasted on them, they are absorbing something, they are, in today's ghastly jargon, exposed to it, as though it were some pernicious infection. Remember, a well-loved children's book is read and read again—half a dozen times is not unusual—so that the phrases sink deep into the mind at its most impressionable. How many adult books get even a second reading? Also, despite television and transistors, the tradition of reading aloud to children is by no means dead. To be read aloud is no bad test of prose. It is a challenge to the author to do his work well.

He is not really handicapped in his vocabulary, and should not let himself be frightened into feeling so. Some of our best and also most popular children's authors command a wealth of language—I think of Leon Garfield—that makes many contemporary novels seem impoverished. Children respond to the unfamiliar word, if it is exotic, musical or evocative, so long as the story has the vitality to sweep them along. Sensible teachers encourage the storyteller to use the vocabulary he needs. 'Go on,' they say, 'how else will our children ever learn new words?' If we thus happen, incidentally, to become 'teacher's aid', we are delighted. But it must *be* incidentally. The story must be our own free spontaneous creation, never something self-consciously tailored to fit classroom requirements—easy to say but not always easy to hold to in an age when, at least until the recent economies, publishers have come to rely upon the educational authorities as the big spenders.

It is not always recognised what pressures have been exerted by the educational theorists, especially in this matter of vocabulary. Margery Fisher has said:

> I think the writer of children's books is the most harried and impeded . . . We are all familiar with the attempts of the late Miss Blyton to have Beatrix Potter rewritten so that the kiddies can understand her. But . . . we are just as guilty if we ask that a book of personal vision should be carried out within word limits, or if we provide a difficult future for a writer by suggesting that he has used words too difficult for his supposed readership.

She tells a story against herself. She was picking out books for a grand-daughter, then a late reader of nearly eight. 'I was thinking,' she says, 'in theoretical terms . . . "Ah, yes, reluctant reader, repetition to help her along," and I found an easy book with a repetitive pattern. When she came to the fourth repetition of words and situations she heaved a great sigh and said, "Not again." So I left her by the bookshelf.'

Vocabulary limitation became a fashion in America about fifty years ago, and was taken up in this country after the second World War. Publishers were intimidated—or tempted—and began to urge it upon authors. A cry went up: 'Books for the reluctant reader!' No one dared say 'backward'—that was already going the same way as a number of other honest but uncomfortable words. Some publishers' editors, again following American tendencies, tried to assume more and more power over the final form of the text. A defeatist attitude gained ground. Bruno Bettelheim, in a recently published study, *On Learning to Read*, has analysed American reading primers and found that the number of different words used has been halved since the cult of vocabulary limitation came in. Yet Helen Keller, at only six years old, blind and deaf, learned 400 words on the palm of her hand in the course of a few weeks. 'By now,' says Bettelheim, 'several generations of American primary-grade children have been cheated out of discovering that reading is the most stimulating, rewarding and meaningful experience school has to offer them.' These reading primers, we are told, are homogenised, emulsified, bleached and pre-digested, with added non-racism and non-sexism—junk books. They are, admittedly, published for class use, but what starts in the schoolbook has a habit of spreading to children's literature in general. Just as what starts in America has a habit of spreading to Britain.

As, for instance, the pressure group. Its development threatens a new form of censorship, more organised and more ideological than the prejudices that hampered children's writers in days gone by. Already we see, stealing in, the 'guide-lines' that recommend the words we should use—not 'housewife' but 'home-maker', not 'fireman' but 'fire-fighter'. There is a new kind of criticism that assesses children's books not by literary criteria but by their possible contribution to women's liberation or the building of a multiracial society. Whatever an author's views on those matters he wishes to remain independent, not to be conscripted as a social engineer. The well-known *Ladybird* series may not be of great artistic merit—but should it be fiercely denounced because it shows 'a white middle-class world peopled with daddies in suits and mummies in frilly aprons, who take tea on lawns in front of their detached houses'? The implied venom concentrated in that short sentence would arouse envy in the healthiest rattlesnake. The depiction of such a world, we are assured, is 'likely to be irrelevant and harmful for urban working-class and black children.'

It is easy to smile at these denunciations, made by a small, if strident, minority—but they can frighten a timid publisher who feels, in hard times, that a single hostile teacher is one too many. A well-known children's storyteller told me some years ago that her latest manuscript had been strongly criticised by her editor for being too 'middle-class'—a term which is becoming in some quarters a synonym for 'obscene'. I myself once wrote an eighteenth-century story in which the hero was a chocolate boy, one of those black pages who used to serve the ladies of Georgian England with that fashionable beverage. But hero though he was, and depicted with my warmest sympathy, he was dynamite to the nervous editor. She had been hearing about the pressure groups. She said she liked the story but dared not publish it. Ethnic minorities did not wish to be reminded of bygone servitude. Historical accuracy was no justification, and even my sympathetic presentation of the little boy would be discounted as patronising. 'The Uncle Tom syndrome', I believe it is called. This editor was unnecessarily timid. The book came out under another imprint, and went into paperback, and not a word of complaint has ever reached me. But an author might easily have been discouraged and tried no further.

We should not overrate the power of these pressure groups. The danger is that some publishers may. Countless children—including black children, the librarians assure us—are still enjoying *Little Black Sambo*, as their parents and grandparents did before them—and this in spite of a virulent campaign against the book in some quarters. And I can still see on my marmalade pot at breakfast the jolly little figure I have known ever since I can remember. But the price of liberty here, as elsewhere, is eternal vigilance.

I began by acknowledging the material benefits children's writers have received from the use of their books in schools during their precarious lives. Many have been teachers, some still are, and all but a few extreme individualists are in sympathy with education. They are happy if teachers find their books useful, sorry but philosophical if they do not. But they want the teachers to judge and choose from the books when they are published. They do not want to write to specification or under duress, or to be assessed on any grounds but merit. From which it follows that they would prefer a little more attention from the students of literature, a little less from the educational theorists.

I will end with a comment made by C. S. Lewis, himself no mean figure in both scholarship and storytelling: 'I will not say that a good children's book could never be written by some one in the Ministry of Education, but I should lay very long odds against it.'

J. J. ROUSSEAU AND THE BIRTH OF ROMANTICISM

MAURICE CRANSTON FRSL

Read 10th February 1983:
John Guest, FRSL, in the Chair

ROUSSEAU has returned in recent years to public esteem. Between the two wars, he was condemned by right and left alike, seen as the forerunner at once of fascism and of communism, an enemy of science and of reason, responsible both for the excesses of romanticism and the French revolution, a mountebank and a freak, sick in the mind. Fashions, however, change in philosophy as in clothes, and events have conspired to make many of the main themes of Rousseau's writings disturbingly topical. The invention of nuclear weapons has undermined faith in the benevolence of science; the pollution of nature by industry has made people question the virtues of technology; the enlargement of bureaucracy has thwarted men's hopes of participatory democracy, and the freedom which the victory of 1945 promised seems to have brought with it new constraints and burdens almost everywhere. We are acutely aware today of problems which Rousseau in the eighteenth century was almost alone in discerning.

This renewed popularity has, however, its negative aspect; there is a danger of Rousseau being transformed from a philosopher into an ideologue, the prophet of the alienated, the inspiration of revolutionary yearnings, nourishing imaginative minds with visions of an ideal state. Paradoxically, this is just the impact which Rousseau wished not to have. He sought not to propel men forward to revolution, but to urge them to retrace their steps, and recover the moral virtues which had been valued in the ancient world.

The eighteenth century was a progressive age. The great *Encyclopédie* which Rousseau's best friend Diderot[1] edited, and for which he himself wrote many articles, was fully and enthusiastically committed to the doctrine of development in technology, art, commerce and industry. 'Science will save us' was the motto not only of Diderot, but of all the *philosophes* who dominated the Enlightenment. However, at the age of 37, Rousseau had what he called an 'illumination' on the road to Vincennes while walking to visit Diderot who had been imprisoned there on charges of injuring religion in the interests of science. Rousseau says it came to him in a terrible flash that the arts and sciences had corrupted instead of improving men's morals; and he promptly lost all his faith in progress. He went on to write his first important publication, his *Discourse on the Arts and Sciences*, in which he argued that the history of culture had been a history of decay. This *Discourse* is by no means Rousseau's best work, but its central theme was to inform almost everything else he wrote throughout his life; he kept coming back to the idea that man is good by nature and has been corrupted by society and civilisation. Rousseau did not say that society and civilisation were inherently bad, but rather that both had taken a wrong direction and become harmful as they had become more advanced and more sophisticated.

This idea in itself was not unfamiliar when Rousseau published his *Discourses on the Arts and Sciences* in 1749. Many Christians, especially Catholics, deplored the direction that European culture had taken since the middle ages. Disapproving of the Renaissance, the Reformation, and the rise of science and industry, such readers shared the hostility towards progress that Rousseau expressed, even if they did not share his belief that man is naturally good. But it was just his belief in natural goodness that Rousseau regarded as the most important part of his argument and this idea, as he developed it, set him even further apart both from the progressives and the reactionaries. Even so, he remained for several years after the publication of his first

---

[1] Denis Diderot (1713–1784), born and bred in Langres, a cutler's son, was a year younger than Rousseau. He met him in Paris soon after they both arrived there as young aspiring writers seeking fame in the metropolis. His greatest achievement was editing the *Encyclopédie* in thirty-five large volumes.

Discourse a close collaborator with Diderot, and one of the most active contributors to successive volumes of the *Encyclopédie*.

Rousseau's speciality on the *Encyclopédie* was music, and it was in this sphere that he first established his influence as a reformer. His early writings on music are not well known; they have not been translated into English, and the world seems to have forgotten the importance they had at the time they were published. Rousseau's *Confessions* contains a paragraph which has puzzled many readers: 'In 1753, the *parlement* of Paris had just been exiled by the King; unrest at its height; all the signs pointed to an early uprising. My *Letter on French Music* was published, and all other quarrels were immediately forgotten. No one thought of anything but the danger to French music, and the only uprising that took place was against me. The conflict was so fierce that the nation was never to recover from it . . . If I say that my writings may have averted a political revolution in France, people will think me mad; nevertheless, it is a very real truth'.[1]

It is ironical that the philosopher most often named as being responsible for the French revolution should have seen himself as a man who prevented a revolution taking place in France, but there is no reason to think him mad for making the claim. The attempt of Louis XV in 1753 to dissolve the great chamber of the Paris *parlement* and replace it with a Royal Chamber met with such furious resistance that the capital appeared to responsible observers to be on the brink of a rebellion.[2] It was not a rebellion to command the sympathy of Rousseau or Diderot or anyone else connected with the *Encyclopédie*. The Paris *parlements* were judiciary bodies, not to be confused with parliaments on the English model, where representatives of the people sit to legislate: the *parlements* were composed of lawyers, often more eager than the royal government at Versailles to defend the Church and suppress books of the kind that the *Encyclopédistes* wrote. As between the King and the *parlements*, the typical free-thinking French intellectual or *philosophe* was disposed to prefer the former.

But is it conceivable that a dispute about music could have diverted aggression that would otherwise have gone into a political rebellion? Others besides Rousseau believed it. Mercier in his *Tableau de Paris*

---

[1] J. J. Rousseau *Oeuvres Complètes*, Ed. Gagnebin and Raymond, Paris, 1959, I p. 384.

[2] See R. Wokler in *Studies in the Eighteenth Century* Ed. Brissendon and Eade, Canberra, 1979 pp. 251–283.

wrote 'The operatic factions made all other factions disappear'.[1] And Melchior Grimm, in his *Correspondence Littéraire*, reported that the French public was 'much more interested in the quarrel provoked by Rousseau's *Letter* than by the affair of the Royal Chamber'.[2] Culture was taken seriously in eighteenth-century Paris, and a quarrel about music had already been brewing when Rousseau burst into print on the subject. This dispute, known at the time as the *querelle des Bouffons* or war of the opera companies, dated from the arrival in Paris in the summer of 1752 of an Italian opera company to perform works of *opera buffa* (hence the name *'Bouffon'*) by Pergolesi, Scarlatti, Vinci, Leo and other such composers new to France. This event promptly divided the French music-loving public into two excited camps, supporters of the new Italian opera against supporters of the familiar French opera. The *Encyclopédistes* entered the fray as champions of Italian music, and Rousseau, who knew more about Italian music than the others after the months he spent haunting the opera houses of Venice when he was attached to the French Embassy there in 1743 and 1744, and who was the leading expert on musical subjects for the *Encyclopédie*, emerged as the most forceful and effective combatant, a leader of a little army of pamphleteers. He was the only one to direct his fire squarely at the leading living exponent of French music, Rameau, and he kept up the controversy with Rameau long after the Italian opera company had packed their bags and departed from Paris.

Rousseau was quick to realise that the *querelle des Bouffons* was as much an ideological as a musical one. This is what gave him the advantage over Rameau. For Rameau, already in his seventieth year in 1752, was not only the leading composer of French opera, he was, as the author of a *Treatise on Harmony* and other technical treatises, Europe's leading musicologist. His prestige as a theorist of music matched his popularity as a creative musician. Rousseau, by contrast, was a newcomer to music, with no professional training, no standing, and no authority. In the end, none of these factors hindered his triumph. Rousseau entered the dispute as a reformer against a conservative; and it was a reformer of musical taste that he made his first real mark in the world.

The French opera that Rameau defended was not simply national, it was traditional, authoritarian, academic. Its intellectual complexity

[1] *Tableau de Paris*, Amsterdam, 1783, VII. p. 269.
[2] *Correspondance Littéraire*. Ed. Tourneux, Paris, 1877, I pp. 313–314.

had much in common with Descartes' philosophy of mathematical elaboration and rational order; its pomp expressed the self-esteem of the French kings. Moreover, the *libretti* of French operas proclaimed the same Cartesian principles of order and the same Bourbon myth of *gloire*, the splendour of earthly princes being represented on the stage in the image of Gods. Superior beings were impersonated by the actors, and celebrated with the kind of music which appealed, with its intricate harmonies, to superior minds, or which evoked martial feelings by the sound of trumpets and drums. French opera spoke to the ear in the same manner in which the architecture of Versailles appealed to the eye.

In all these respects, the Italian *opera buffa* was different from the French. It was not imposing; it was pleasing. In place of *déclamation*, it introduced arias or songs. And whereas French operatic music was both pompous and highbrow, the Italian was tuneful and simple. Almost anyone could sing the arias of an Italian opera, and in Naples and Venice almost everyone did. The themes of *opera buffa* were domestic and familiar; instead of Gods and Kings, ordinary people occupied the stage. Pergolesi's *La Serva padrona*, with which the Italian company opened their season in Paris and which Rousseau himself edited for publication in France, is about bourgeois bachelor being driven by jealousy into marrying his maid. One can well imagine that even the plot of this opera might alarm conservatives in Paris, if such people took seriously the moral of the tale, that a maid is as good as her mistress.

Rousseau built up his case for the superiority of Italian music over French on one central principle: that melody must have priority over harmony. Rameau took the opposite position—asserting that harmony must have priority over melody. Now this is not a mere technical point, as both disputants realised. Rousseau, pleading for melody, was asserting what came to be recognised as a central belief of romanticism: namely that the free expression of the creative spirit in art is more important than strict adhesion to formal rules and technical precision. Rameau, pleading for harmony, was reaffirming the first principle of French classicism—that conformity to rationally intelligible principles is a necessary condition of true art.

In music Rousseau was a liberator. He not only argued for freedom in music in his pamphlets, he proved the possibility of adapting the Italian style of music to the French theatre in a little opera he composed himself: *Le Devin du village*. This work not only had an immense success before the royal family at Fontainebleau and with the public in Paris, it proved an inspiration for later composers. Gluck, who succeeded Rameau as the most important operatic composer in France, acknowledged his debt to Rousseau's teaching and example. Mozart based his *Bastien and Bastienne* on Rousseau's *Devin du village*. Rousseau had propelled European music into new channels: he put an end to the age of classicism, and initiated an age of romanticism.

But having composed *Le Devin du village* Rousseau decided to turn aside from composing music.[1] He would go on writing articles about musical subjects, and copying other people's music as a means of earning a living, but his creative talents he decided to devote henceforth entirely to literature and philosophy. It was all part of his 'reform' or improvement of his own character; a process which took him back to some of the austere principles that had been instilled in him as a child in the Calvinist republic of Geneva.

The political structure of Geneva was unique in Europe, and no one can understand what Rousseau felt and said about politics without paying attention to the peculiar circumstances of the political education he received. In the middle of the sixteenth century, the townsfolk of Geneva, who had been ruled for generations by a dual principate of Counts and Bishops, were given so many powers by the Bishop in his efforts to overcome the Count, that they contrived to turn those powers against the giver, outwit the Bishop as he had outwitted the Count, and proclaim themselves sovereigns over their own city. However, the people quarrelled so much among themselves, that their democratic constitution soon ceased to function democratically, and the upper-class families took possession of all public offices. The population was increasingly composed of French Protestant refugees, and Calvin himself appeared among them at a critical moment almost as a Law-giver, providing Geneva with a constitution in which democracy and aristocracy and theocracy were curiously balanced, and with institutions to ensure that government was honest and private morality upheld. Calvin's Protestantism was so fanatical, however, that the Catholic cantons refused to admit Geneva to the

---

[1] He did not resume composition again until later life, when he devised in collaboration with Corancez a four-act *pastorale* called *Daphnis et Cloé* and several dozen fragments of vocal music. He had argued vigorously in his *Letter on French Music* that the French language was so corrupt, so far removed from its origins as a system of natural communication between men that French words could not be set to music.

Swiss Confederation, so that the city had to remain an independent state despite its having a population of less than 25,000 people.

The Genevans consoled themselves with the thought that their little city was a free republic, like the cities of antiquity, as noble and splendid as Rome. Rousseau heard a great deal of this sort of talk when he was a boy. His father was a fervent patriot, and he encouraged him to read Plutarch and other classical authors who proclaimed the value of 'republican virtues': courage, heroism, endurance, devotion, honour. 'I believed myself to be a Greek or a Roman'.[1] Rousseau wrote in *Emile*, looking back on his childhood. On another occasion he wrote: 'At twelve I was a Roman'.[2]

What Rousseau seems to have been unaware of when he was young was that there were profound political dissensions beneath all these appearances of 'Roman' freedom and splendour in the Genevan city state. Every adult male citizen—and there were about 1,500 of them when Rousseau was boy—had, in principle, a share in the sovereignty of the republic and a right to participate and vote at meetings of the General Assembly. In effect, despite Calvin's constitution, the old patriciate prevailed; all decisions were taken by the Small Council which recruited its members exclusively from a few rich families—all living in elegant houses on the top of the hill. This Small Council, which was supposed to be the administrative body, had in effect become also the sovereign body of Geneva. The constitution was a facade; although there were some citizens—including, it seems, Rousseau's father—who chose not to see it as a facade. There were others, liberals or champions of citizens rights, who at different periods were openly or covertly trying to recover the lost rights of the ordinary citizens; but in the years immediately before Rousseau's birth this liberal movement had been suppressed by the execution of its leaders, and Rousseau grew up at a time of tranquillity, when the conservative propaganda of the patrician regime went unchallenged.

Rousseau remained in most respects conservative in his politics. He kept his idealised vision of the character of the Genevan state until his fifties; and then, dismayed at being persecuted by the regime as a result of the publication of *Emile* and *The Social Contract*—books condemned in Geneva as irreligious—he attacked the government while continuing to plead for national unity. Even in his strongest attack on the regime, his *Letters from the Mountains*, a pamphlet

[1] *Oeuvres complètes*, IV p. 535.
[2] *op. cit.* I p. 1036.

written at the prompting of his friends in the liberal and radical factions, Rousseau condemns all factions, and urges his readers in Geneva to think and act together as patriots.

Rousseau's most 'revolutionary' publication his *Discourse on the Origins of Inequality* is dedicated to Geneva; and he always claimed that his *Social Contract* was inspired by the constitution of Geneva. Geneva lies at the heart of all his thinking about politics. Empires, kingdoms and principalities—constitutions of the kind which were standard form in almost all parts of the world when Rousseau was born in 1712—were alien to him. As a result of this he had many ideas about politics which to others seemed strange or unintelligible or were simply misunderstood.

One of the most important of these ideas was Rousseau's conception of freedom. He was passionately devoted to freedom, but freedom meant something different to him from what it meant to almost everyone else. People who talked about liberty in France, or England or America meant the right of the individual to do what he wanted to do, provided it was lawful; freedom was freedom from the constraints of the state. For Rousseau freedom was the freedom the people of Geneva had obtained when they expelled the ruling Bishop in the sixteenth century, the right to participate in the making of the laws, the right to rule themselves.

This distinction between Rousseau's concept of freedom and that of other people was very clearly detected by Benjamin Constant,[1] a fellow Swiss, but a Swiss from the canton of Vaud, accustomed only to being ruled by the Dukes of Savoy or the equally alien magistrates of Berne. Benjamin Constant said Rousseau did not understand 'modern freedom', but always thought in terms of 'ancient freedom'—freedom as it was known in Greek city-states or the Roman republic, when freedom meant not 'being allowed to do what you want to do', but 'participating actively in the legislation of the city'. Constant suggested that Rousseau was ruinously misguided in trying to revive in the modern world this ancient concept of freedom. Why ruinously? Because if the state were thought of something that expressed my will then I would have no motive for writing to diminish the activity of the state, and might well want to enlarge it. Constant feared that the cause of freedom, which was seen by those who thought of 'modern freedom', as requiring curbs and checks being placed on the powers of

---

[1] Benjamin Constant (1767–1830) author of *Principes de politiques, De l'Esprit de couquête*, etc.

the state for the protection of the individual was a cause that would be abandoned by people who thought of freedom on the model 'ancient freedom', and whose purpose was simply to make the state their own.

This is a fair criticism. For Rousseau the political independence of Geneva was a good thing, despite the tiny size of Geneva in the eighteenth-century—which many Genevans in the seventeenth-century regretted because they feared themselves too vulnerable in being left outside the Swiss confederation, and which their successors in the nineteenth-century ended by securing admission to that Confederation—that 'weakness' of Geneva Rousseau saw as its merit. For only in a small community, in a 'face-to-face society' can all the citizens meet to make the laws they live under; and hence, if we follow Rousseau's conception of freedom, it is only in a small community that men can experience freedom. The theory of freedom which he develops in depth in his *Social Contract* is simply not applicable to the large scale empires, kingdoms and principalities within which most Westerners lived. It could not even apply to Venice, which had grown from a city to the size of a small empire. It made no sense at all in France, where the population was 25 million.

And yet the French and other foreigners feasted on Rousseau's ideas. Or should we rather say, that they feasted on his eloquence? Few of them saw what Constant saw, that when Rousseau wrote of '*liberté*', he meant something sharply opposed to what their own philosophers meant by '*liberté*'. It seems equally improbable that Rousseau's readers really grasped what he meant by 'equality', another word which he propelled into the forefront of ideological language.

His *Discourse on the Origins of Inequality* is a masterpiece of speculative anthropology. It follows up the argument of his first *Discourse*, which stresses the theme that modern civilisation is bad, by developing the proposition that natural man is good, and by tracing the successive stages by which man has descended from primitive innocence to sophisticated corruption. The *Discourse on Inequality* is remarkable achievement. In less than a hundred pages, Rousseau outlined a theory of evolution which prefigured the discoveries of Darwin, opened new channels for the study of linguistics, and made a seminal contribution to political and economic thought.

He begins his enquiry by noting that there are two kinds of inequality among men: the first are natural inequalities, arising from differences in strength, intelligence and so forth; the second are artificial inequalities deriving from the conventions which govern society. It is the inequalities of the latter sort that he proposes to investigate, and ask if they are ethically justifiable. Adopting what he considered the properly 'scientific' method of studying a phenomenon by research into its origins in time, he tries to reconstruct the first phases, or pre-history, of human societies. He suggests that original man was not social but solitary; and to this extent Rousseau agrees with Hobbes's account of the state of nature, but against Hobbes's view that the life of man in such a state must be 'poor, nasty, brutish and short', Rousseau claims that original man, though admittedly solitary, is healthy, happy, good and free. The vices of men, Rousseau claims, date from the time when each entered into society and began to compare himself with his neighbours, to compete and covet and desire to dominate.

Thus Rousseau blames society, and exonerates nature from responsibility for men's vices. Passions, which hardly exist in the state of nature, develop in society. It is 'the calm of their own passions and their ignorance of vice'[1] which preserve savages from evil. Society began when man started to build huts, which facilitated co-habitation; and, later, from co-habitation there arose the habit of living as a family and associating with neighbours. 'Nascent society', as Rousseau calls it, was good: it was the golden age of man. But it did not last. Neighbours started to compare their achievements one with another: and this 'marked the first step towards inequality, and at the same time, towards vice'.[2]

Men started to demand consideration and respect: their innocent self-love became a culpable pride as everyone wanted to be better than everyone else. The institution of property marked another decisive step towards modern inequality. In the primitive state, according to Rousseau, the earth belonged to everybody or to nobody; but when agriculture was invented, an inevitable consequence was a claim being made for the rightful ownership of the piece of land which a particular farmer had cultivated, and this introduced the 'fatal'[3] concept of property. Property, in turn, entailed institutions of law and government: 'the first man who enclosed a piece of land and took it upon himself to say "This is mine", and found people simple enough to believe him, was the true founder of civil society. What crimes, what

[1] *Oeuvres complètes* III p. 151.
[2] *op. cit.* p. 169.
[3] *op. cit.* p. 171.

wars, what murders, what miseries, what horrors the human race might have been spared if someone had pulled up the stakes and filled in the ditch crying out to his fellow men "Beware of this imposter: you are lost if you forget that the fruits belong to all, and the earth to no one".[1]

This is inflammatory language: and one can readily imagine that such passages from Rousseau excited revolutionaries like Ropespierre and Lenin. But Rousseau is not in fact recommending anyone to 'cry out' today the appeal he would like to have been uttered at an earlier period. He does not suggest this appeal would have any relevance whatever at any other time, than at that moment which marked the passage from 'nascent society' to 'civil society'.

'Civil society' comes into being to serve two purposes: to provide peace for everyone and ensure the right to property for anyone lucky enough to have possessions. In effect it enables the rich to enjoy their riches at the expense of the poor in the context of civil tranquillity. Unfortunately it does not ensure happiness for either rich or poor. The savage, according to Rousseau, has only to eat and he is at peace with nature 'and the friend of all his fellow men'.[2] Man in civil society is never happy because he is never satisfied: 'first it is a question of providing the necessities, then the extras, afterwards come the luxuries, then riches, then subjects, then slaves—there is no letting up'.[3] Society leads men to hate one another in proportion to the conflict between their interests; and 'the universal desire for preference for oneself makes all men enemies'.[4]

It will be noticed that Rousseau treats the inequality between men as one of the characteristics of society, but he does not treat it in isolation. He sees it as one feature of a longer process, the progressive alienation of man from nature and innocence. He is certainly not pleading for equality to be introduced into modern society, since he makes it plain enough that inequality lies at the very roots of society as such.

Nevertheless in the 'Dedication' which he wrote for the *Discourse on Inequality* in order to offer it to the 'Republic of Geneva', Rousseau makes it clear what sorts of equality—and inequality—are desirable in a well-ordered state in the modern world. The arrangement he

[1] *op. cit.* p. 164.
[2] *op. cit.* p. 203.
[3] *ibid.*
[4] *op. cit.* p. 188.

praises in Geneva is similar to that which Plato demanded for his ideal republic: namely one whereby the best men are in the highest places. Again he makes several references to ancient Rome—'that model for all free Peoples'[1]; and then goes on to congratulate Geneva for having its wise men as its magistrates, its virtuous men as its clergy and begs that 'precious half' of the republic, the women folk, to rule the rest, but 'always as chaste wives, on the model of the women of Sparta'.[2] There are no 'egalitarian' sentiments in Rousseau in the sense in which egalitarianism features in later ideologies. He does not even hold with Jefferson, who often responded to Rousseau's influence, that 'all men are born equal'. He holds that they *were* born equal just as they *were* born free. But that was a long time ago. As to the measures of equality and liberty that men might be able to recover in modern civilisation, Rousseau is nowhere very encouraging. Having rejected the doctrine of progress, he could hardly believe that time alone would bring improvement. He left that optimistic thought to the more superficial *Encyclopédistes*, to philosophers like Voltaire. Rousseau had no desire to tell people what they wanted to hear. He wanted only to tell the truth. He believed that *civil* liberty, as distinct from a general liberty, and civil equality, as distinct from social equality, could be obtained in a genuinely republican state: but that such a state can only exist on the strength of the moral virtues of its citizens. Man has lost his natural goodness by entering into society; and to overcome the distinctive passions that society breeds, men must acquire virtues, every man must teach himself to be as disciplined, brave, upright, honest, and patriotic as the ancient Romans.

In his writings on music, Rousseau unveiled the smiling face of romanticism, its promise of freedom from all external constraints that bind the voice of the heart; in his writings on politics he shows us the stern face of romanticism, its demand that a man who is not subservient to others much fiercely govern himself.

---

[1] *op. cit.* p. 113.
[2] *op. cit.* p. 113.

THE LIFE AND EARLY DEATH OF GEORGIANISM

SAMUEL HYNES FRSL

Read 18th March 1982:
Frank Kermode, FBA, FRSL, in the Chair

THE particular occasion for this evening's lecture is the centenary of the birth of John Drinkwater, which occurs this year. Drinkwater had a particularly close connection with the Royal Society of Literature: he was a Fellow for nearly twenty years, from 1918 until his death in 1937; and from 1921 he was Professor of Poetry, an honour conferred by the Society during the years between the wars. I don't know what the privileges of the Professor of Poetry were, but the principal duty was clearly the preparation of a great many lectures: Drinkwater gave twenty-seven during his years with the RSL. So it is altogether appropriate that the Society should take notice of his centenary with yet another lecture—this one on the group of poets of which he was an important member.

Unfortunately for Drinkwater, he must share his centenary year with a number of other notable persons: with James Joyce, Virginia Woolf, and Wyndham Lewis, for example, and with Pavlova, Braque, and Stravinsky; and, to venture a bit further afield, with Franklin Roosevelt, Melanie Klein, Sylvia Pankhurst, Air Chief Marshal Dowding, John Barrymore, and Sam Goldwyn. *These* are the men and women who made our world—our art, our thought, our politics, even our war: the Generation of the 1880s is where Modernism comes from.

But though Drinkwater shared their birthyear, he does not belong in their company. Nor do any of the other principal Georgian Poets with whom his name is customarily linked. Why, then, should we spend an evening considering them? Why speak of *Georgians* in this, the Year of the Moderns?

Well, first of all because they are there in history—a part of the record, though a neglected part. More than most kinds of history, literary history is what Butterfield called *Whig* history; the kind, that is, that looks back to the past to find the forces that produced the present—to establish the genealogy of the way things are now. This means, in effect, noticing the winners and ignoring the losers; in the present instance it means focusing on the origins and growth of modernism in the early years of this century, and neglecting or dismissing the literature that seems to us, in retrospect, *un*-modern. When I told a literary friend of mine that I was going to lecture on the Georgians, he asked anxiously: 'You're not going to say the Poundian revolution was all a mistake, are you?' Well no, I'm not—partly because *revolution* is the wrong word for what Pound and Eliot accomplished, and partly because history doesn't make mistakes. But I *am* going to argue that the history of English poetry during the 'Georgian' years was more than Yeats, Pound and Eliot, and that we will not understand that history properly unless we give some attention to the 'Life and Early Death of Georgianism.'

Let us begin with *Georgian* in its narrowest sense: that is, with the five anthologies titled *Georgian Poetry*, edited by Edward Marsh, that appeared between 1912 and 1922. And since they were Marsh's idea, we must begin with him. In 1912 Marsh was 40 years old, a bachelor and a civil servant (he was Private Secretary to Winston Churchill, who at that time was First Lord of the Admiralty). He was well-educated, comfortably off and socially very acceptable. And he was fond of poetry. There must have been many such young men in England in 1912.

Marsh was, by his own account, a man of very defined poetic tastes:

I was, of course, [he later wrote] guided by the preferences which instinct and training had formed in my mind; and these can be easily, if roughly, set forth. I liked poetry to be all three (or if not all three, at least two; or if the worst came to the worst, at least one) of the following things: intelligible, musical, and racy; and I was happier with it if it was written on some formal principle which I

could discern, and from which it departed, if at all, only for the sake
of some special effect, and not because the lazy or too impetuous
writer had found observance difficult or irksome. I liked poetry that
I wanted to know by heart, and *could* learn by heart if I had time.

And he was persuaded that England in 1912 was pullulating with new
poets who wrote his kind of poetry (he had apparently been reading
Masefield's *Everlasting Mercy* and the *Poems* of Rupert Brooke with
great excitement). And so, with the help of some friends he prepared
and published an anthology of recent poems, to introduce these new
poets to a larger audience.

The Preface (dated October 1912) that Marsh wrote for this first
volume of *Georgian Poetry* is an enthisiastic, and rather touching,
declaration of his faith: 'This volume is issued,' he wrote, 'in the belief
that English poetry is now once again putting on a new strength and
beauty.'

> Few readers have the leisure or the zeal to investigate each volume
> as it appears; and the process or recognition is often slow. This
> collection, drawn entirely from the publications of the past two
> years, may if it is fortunate help the lovers of poetry to realize that
> we are at the beginning of another 'Georgian period' which may
> take rank in due time with the several great poetic ages of the past.

It is difficult, looking back, to understand how anyone could have
chosen 1912 as the beginning of a new era. To us, it must seem that the
turning points in modern poetic history came either earlier or later, or
both—with Hardy and Yeats at the turn of the century, and with
Pound and Eliot after the war. But *1912*? Nevertheless, the fact
remains that in October 1912 a man of literary tastes who was not a
fool thought that a new 'Georgian period' was beginning. And because
he thought so, he called his anthology *Georgian Poetry*.

Let us pause for a moment to take note of the assumptions that
underlie Marsh's preface. First, he is announcing not a poetic revolution, but a recurrence: poetry is *once again* putting on a new strength
and beauty, we are at the beginning of *another* Georgian period. This
theory of periodic renewal is a conservative view of literary history,
but it is a possible one: it implies a continuous tradition (though of
fluctuating vigour), and—most important—a continuous audience.
The 'lovers of poetry' may be busy, and behind in their reading, but
they are always *there*. The anthologist's task is simply to reach them

with the good news: it has to do with publicity and distribution, not with creation, nor even with discovery.

And what was the poetry like that Marsh offered to this audience? One might answer that question simply by naming the principal contributors to the five volumes: Lascelles Abercrombie, Gordon Bottomley, W. H. Davies, Walter de la Mare, John Drinkwater, Wilfrid Wilson Gibson, and Harold Monro (none a household word these days) all appeared in all, or in all but one, of the volumes, and we can regard them as the essential, central Georgians—the proofs, if it is to be proven, of the 'new strength and beauty' in English poetry that Marsh announced. To this list we must add one other, rather surprising name: D. H. Lawrence appeared in every volume except the one published in 1917.

About these eight poets one can make some general observations: that they were roughly of one generation, born in the 1870s or early '80s; that they were mostly of lower or lower-middle class origins; that they had no money, and worked during their early years at pedestrian, unliterary jobs: Abercrombie a quantity surveyor, de la Mare a book-keeper, Lawrence a schoolmaster, Drinkwater an insurance office clerk, Davies a tramp. Only one—Monro—had a university education. Several began their poetic careers by publishing their works at their own expense. Together they represent an assumption about the social origins, and perhaps also about the social *role*, of poetry: that it has nothing to do with education, or unusual learning, or knowledge of foreign literary traditions or languages; that ordinary people make it, and that they make it *for* ordinary people. Davies' practice of printing his poems as broadsheets, and hawking them from door to door for a penny, is an extreme case of this assumption in practice, but I think they all shared it in principle. (And it is, obviously, the opposite of what we think of as Modernism.)

The poems that they made on this principle were familiar-looking poems. One could describe them in various ways: formally, they are virtually all in familiar, unadventurous verse forms—many in blank verse, a number of sonnets, some rhymed quatrains (the only poem in the five volumes that is neither metrical nor rhymed is Lawrence's 'Snake'; anyone who had read a bit in Palgrave would feel at home in *Georgian Poetry*. One could say that these are poems located in nature or in myth, but never in history; that many are narrative or dramatic —story-telling, anecdotal poems, and that others are celebrations of sensory experiences of the natural world. On the whole they seem to be based on the assumption that nothing specifically modern or urban *can* be poetical, and that virtually everything in nature *must* be. Described in these terms (and in this tone), *Georgian Poetry* sounds like no more than tired Romanticism—not the beginning of *another* 'Georgian period', but the fag-end of the previous one.

Certainly country matters were a recurrent subject. *Take now a country mood*, a poem, by Robert Graves begins:

> Take now a country mood,
> Resolve, distil it:—

And so they did. They distilled their country moods, they described them, they named their country parts. They named English places: Twm Barlum, Devil's Edge, Hawkshaw Head, Malpas Bank; Whipham, Week, Watchet, Wye, Withy, Wellover, Wassop, Wo (all those Ws are from de la Mare's 'Off the Ground': Royston, Trumpington, Ditton, Harston, Shelford, Barton, Coton, Madingley, Cherry Hinton (these are all from Brooke's 'The Old Vicarage Granchester') And the things of nature—trees and animals and birds. Nichols remarked of the fourth volume that it was a very arboreal book; but he might with equal justice have described it as very *avian*—J. C. Squire names twenty-one species of English birds in only five lines of a poem. And they named English country characters. Let me just run through the cast of characters of Abercrombie's play 'The End of the World', in the 1913–1915 volume: Huff, the Farmer; Sollers, the Wainwright, Merrick the Smith, Vine, the Publican, Shale, the Labourer, A Dowser, Mrs Huff, Warp, the Molecatcher. We are somewhere between Shakespeare's rustics and *Cold Comfort Farm*; but wherever we are, we aren't in the modern world.

It's not that these poets were born countrymen, writing of what they had always known, or that they were constant country-dwellers (if you recall those jobs I listed, they were most of them city-jobs). No, it was rather that they took country matters to be the necessary and appropriate materials of poetry. This was true even when they turned to town-subjects. Consider as an example Drinkwater's 'A Town Window'.

> Beyond my window in the night
> Is but the drab inglorious street,
> Yet there the frost and clean starlight
> As over Warwick woods are sweet.

> Under the grey drift of the town
> The crocus works among the mould
> As eagerly as those that crown
> Warwick spring in flame and gold.
>
> And when the tramway down the hill
> Across the cobbles moans and rings,
> There is about my window-sill
> The tumult of a thousand wings.

This is an urban scene, right enough, but it is authenticated as poetry by being related to the truly poetical country-images of starlight, flowers, and birds. The country-poem from the city is, of course, a traditional Romantic kind (one can find examples in the works of Wordsworth and Yeats, among many others). But somehow such poems from Georgian hands convinced their detractors that there was something spurious in their relations with the natural world. 'Weekend Wordsworthians' they were called—and not without some justification. It was surely a strategic (as well as a poetic) error on Monro's part to write a public poem titled 'Week-end' that begins:

> The train! the twelve o'clock for paradise.
> Hurry, or it will try to creep away.
> Out in the country every one is wise:
> We can be only wise on Saturday.

Such feelings are familiar enough—for most of us in the twentieth century country-nature *is* a week-end affair; but to write about it in this vein is perhaps a bit too revealing. The country, seen through such week-enders' eyes, would necessarily be a literary scene. Hence the well-known parody of a Georgian poem:

> I sing of green September
> In England's leafy lanes
> In lines that I remember
> From other poets' brains.

Familiar poems, then—even the first reading. And that is the essential case against the Georgians: that their poems were too comfortable, because they had all been done before; that they were simply imitation-Romantic poems; and that the world they rendered was a familiar *literary* world, and not the *un*familiar twentieth-century reality that we all must live in.

But before we join in the general dismissal, we might consider what it is that these poems, and poems like them, actually *do* when they are at their best. Most fundamentally, they celebrate what *is*, assuming that *being* is both constant and knowable—that Twm Barlum will always be Twm Barlum. That's the point in the naming of places and creatures, and in the natural particulars in poems like Graves' *Fox's Dingle*. The dramatic and narrative poems do something similar: they assume that *character* is also constant and knowable, and that *story* —that is, a significant order perceivable in events—is possible. These assumptions are not viewed with favour by contemporary philosophers, but they are the assumptions on which we live our ordinary daily lives; and poems like those of the Georgians seem to claim their place in ordinary living too.

There is another kind of celebration in poems like these that is more difficult to define: but perhaps one could say that simply by existing such poems celebrate the act of celebration itself. It's not just that by writing a sonnet you celebrate the sonnets that already exist, though that is true; it's also that by writing a poem that names things you demonstrate once more than a relationship exists between language and reality—a relationship that all existing poems affirm.

All of these kinds of celebration—of the forms of imagination, of reality, and of language as the connection between them—are, I take it, traditional functions of literature (or functions of traditional literature). They are, no doubt, comforting to the common reader —not because they tell heart-easing things, but because they confirm the common sense of the world. Not every poem in a traditional mode is a good poem, of course, or an interesting or intelligent one; but I can see no obstacle in theory to some of them being worth knowing about.

Ordinariness, I have been suggesting, is at the heart of Georgian poetry. It is more than a matter of style, more even than content: it represents an idea of the relationship between poetry and society, between the poet and his audience—a relationship that assumes community and continuity in literary experience. One may be tempted to translate these terms as middle-classness, or middle-browness —the too easy companionship of the familiar and undemanding. But I don't think this will quite do, not for the best of Georgian poetry, nor for other poems of the larger tradition to which the Georgians belong. That such a poet-audience relationship existed during the Georgian years is certain: after all, *somebody* bought 73,000 volumes of *Georgian Poetry* over the ten years of its existence. So Eddy Marsh's preference for poetry that was intelligible, musical, and racy must have touched a responsive chord in a very large part of the poetry-reading public of those years—though not always in the critical part of that public.

And then, in the midst of the anthologies' success, came the War: a social force of the greatest possible magnitude; but also a *literary* force, which altered sensibilities and re-shaped imagination, and which put a no-man's land between the present and the past. The War must have had a particularly powerful effect, one would have thought, on this conservative group of pre-war poets. But in fact the contents of *Georgian Poetry* changed surprisingly little from pre-war to post-war. The principal Georgians went on writing in much the same style, about much the same things. None of them had much direct contact with the actual fighting of the war, and none of them seems to have experienced that sense of radical discontinuity that affected so many men of their time. Is this a fundamental negative judgment of their work? Is art *bad* art if it is not altered by the upheavals of history? Should Jane Austen have written about Waterloo? At any rate, the Georgians didn't change.

The War did gradually enter the Georgian anthologies, but only via a new, younger generation of poets, and even then in a curiously Georgian way. The first war-poem in *Georgian Poetry* is Brooke's *The Soldier*, in the 1913–1915 volume. It's an entirely Georgian utterance —a sonnet, full of England, in terms of rather vague and general natural imagery, and with nothing modern in it, no guns, no shells (which is not surprising, of course, since Brooke died en route to Gallipoli, though he had a brief experience of fighting in Belgium). Sassoon first appears in the following volume (1916–1917) with a *Letter Home* to Robert Graves, which manages also to be Georgian, using natural imagery to validate its subject just as Drinkwater had used it in his 'Town Window' to validate a tram. The poem begins

> Here I'm sitting in the gloom
> Of my quiet attic room.
> France goes rolling all around,
> Fledged with forest May has crowned,
> And I puff my pipe, calm-hearted,
> Thinking how the fighting started . . .

It is only with the appearance of Robert Nichols, in the same volume, that one finds what one could think of as *real* war-poetry—poetry, that is, that strives to render actual experiences of war, the sort of trench-impressionism that you get in Owen and Rosenberg. But for every poem about war, in this the only war-time Georgian volume, there are five that could easily have come from the first, pre-war collection.

But though the anthologies did not change much, the audience for them did—it died. It is a commonplace that in World War I a generation was destroyed, and we all know the lost poets of that generation—Owen, Isaac Rosenberg, Sorley, Grenfell, poor mad Ivor Gurney. But it was perhaps even more important for the direction of poetry that a generation of poetry-*readers* died. One can identify the soldier-audience that I'm talking about by reading through any of the war-time anthologies of soldier-verse (not the ones published now, like the *Penguin Book of First World War Poetry*, which select with a post-war eye, but those printed during the war, like E. B. Osborn's *The Muse in Arms*, the best known of them (Vera Brittain sent it to her fiancé). From the particulars given in the 'List of Authors' in *The Muse in Arms*, and from the contents of the poems themselves, one can sketch a profile of the typical soldier-poet. He was probably an officer (more than three quarters of the contributors to Osborn's book were), he was middle- or upper-class, public-school educated (there are poems in the book addressed to Eton, Harrow and Marlborough), perhaps had been up to a university (in which case it was almost certainly Oxford or Cambridge); he was fond of animals, sport, his school, his mother, and his country. And he was also fond of poetry.

Such young men wrote astonishing quantities of verse while on active service—so much, indeed, that one journal, the *Westminster Gazette*, had to publish a notice requesting soldier-poets to stop sending in poems. The poems that they wrote were essentially Georgian: that is, they were in traditional verse forms (many were sonnets, following the example of Brooke, I suppose), full of images of the English countryside, open and uncomplicated in their language, and surprisingly lacking in 'modern' references, even when the subject was war. Familiar poems, you might say, of the sort that Marsh preferred—intelligible, musical, and racy. Of course they were: these young men were of Marsh's world, after all.

Most of their poems were negligible as poetry; but the point to be made is that people who *write* poetry, however badly, are the people who *read* it. These young men constituted a substantial part of *Georgian Poetry*'s audience; and by November 1917, when *The Muse in Arms* was published, nearly half of its soldier-contributors were already dead.

It wasn't only an audience that died in France: an idea of the natural world seemed to die, too; or if it didn't die, it suffered severe and lasting damage. I mean that idea of natural benevolence, and of man's comfortable place in nature, that we call Wordsworthian, or Romantic. This idea of nature is the foundation of much English poetry, and of English landscape painting: the nature of the Western Front seemed to make it untenable. 'It is curious,' T. E. Hulme wrote, 'how the mere fact that in a certain direction there are the German lines, seems to alter the feeling of a landscape.' Those lines ran through what *had* been a countryside, full of the sorts of things that a Georgian might name in a poem, but after years of shelling all that had been virtually erased. 'Spring we do have here,' Herbert Read wrote in a letter from the trenches in 1917, 'but in an abortive sort of way. The felled trees bloom, but for the last time, and forget-me-nots spring up among the ruins. But everything is sad, and our few flowers are like wreaths among so much desolation.'

Perhaps the ultimate expression of this sense of the death of Romantic landscape is a painting by Paul Nash (a great friend of the Georgian poets). The painting is of a No-Man's-Land scene: in the foreground the earth is torn and heaped in unnatural mounds and fissures, and farther back broken, dead stumps of trees thrust up into a featureless sky. Over the whole scene a cold light shines from a rising (or is it a setting?) sun. *Nothing* is alive there. Nash titled the picture: *We are making a New World*. In that New World, who would believe in natural benevolence? And who would write, or read, poems about it? If the war had made a new, un-natural world, and if it had destroyed a generation, then surely poetry would have to be different.

But Marsh was reluctant to accept that this should be so. A year after the Armistice he was back with another Georgian volume, which he introduced with a brief but aggressive Prefatory Note.

> This is the fourth volume of the present series [he wrote]. I hope it may be thought to show that what for want of a better word is called Peace has not interfered with the writing of good poetry.

By which of course he meant *his* kind of poetry. Indeed Peace had not interfered with the writing of good poetry; but it seemed to have encouraged a new *kind*. One might have said in defence of Marsh's first volume in 1912 that though it seems a bit conventional and dull to us, it *was* representative of the work that the younger poets of the time were doing—where else could Marsh have gone in 1912 and found better work? But in 1919 a new avante-garde was already in place (in the pages of the Sitwells' *Wheels*, and in many new anthologies and journals): the Sitwells, Huxley, Eliot, Pound, Aldington, H. D. —they were all visible, and if they nevertheless did not appear in the pages of *Georgian Poetry*, it was simply because Marsh didn't like them. He chose to augment his poetic stock instead with poems by Francis Brett Young, Edward Shanks, John Freeman, and J. C. Squire—second-generation Georgians who were simply imitators of the first generation. Osbert Sitwell retaliated with a fierce satire, 'The Jolly Old Squire, or Way Down in Georgia,' and *Georgian* was on the way to becoming a pejorative term, a synonym for mediocre, old-fashioned, imitative, plain boring.

But it wasn't simply its contents that doomed *Georgian Poetry* after the War: it had two other serious disadvantages—it had existed *before* the War, and it was still edited by a man who had been an official member of the pre-war Establishment. It belonged, that is, to the Edwardian world, the world of the Old Men who (in post-war mythology) had made the war. But more than that, it belonged to a past that, to post-war eyes, was *dead*. One of the war-time and post-war commonplaces was that a 'civilisation' had died in the war; and *Georgian Poetry* was the voice in verse of that civilisation.

That sense of the radical historical changes that the war had brought is the subject of some of the most powerful poems of the immediate post-war years—poems like Yeats' *Second Coming* for example, and Eliot's *Waste Land*. But history was not a possible Georgian subject: for the Georgians, poetry was language *not* containing history; its subject was what did *not* change. Even the War they treated not as a case of change, but rather as an interruption of the changeless flow of existence. Thus Nichols, in mid-war, could write:

> For earth yet keeps her undersong
> Of comfort and of ultimate peace,
> That whoso seeks shall never cease
> To hear at dawn or noon or night.

Nothing has really changed, the war was only a temporary madness, the earth abides. But you can't write about the death of a civilisation in such terms.

Marsh soldiered on with one more volume, in 1922, but by then he and his books were under heavy attack, and his Preface is self-defensive—and revealing. 'When the fourth volume of this series was published three years ago,' he wrote:

> many of the critics who had up till then, as Horace Walpole said of God, been the dearest creatures in the world to me, took another turn. Not only did they very properly disapprove my choice of poems: they went on to write as if the Editor of *Georgian Poetry* were a kind of public functionary, like the President of the Royal Academy, and they asked—again, on this assumption, very properly—who was E. M. that he should bestow and withhold crowns and sceptres, and decide that this or that poet was or was not to count.

Marsh's defence was simply that he was a private citizen trying to do a good turn both to the poets and to the reading public, and that he must have succeeded, since people bought the books. But this hardly answered the charge: he *had* in fact for ten years been offering anthologies that professed to represent the time, but that in reality represented only his own taste.

Marsh went on in his Preface to confront the charge that *Georgian Poetry* had merely encouraged a small clique of mutually indistinguishable poetasters. 'It is natural,' he replied:

> that the poets of a generation should have points in common; but to my fond eye those who have graced these collections look as diverse as sheep to their shepherds, or the members of a Chinese family to their uncle.

Could he have understood what he was saying? Did he pause to consider what sheep look like to non-shepherds, or Chinese nephews to non-uncles? What he was actually confessing was the very uniformity that his critics had complained of. Furthermore, his claim that the books represented one poetic generation was not true, and never really had been. In the last, 1920–1922 volume the oldest contributor, W. H. Davies, was over fifty; the youngest, the precocious Peter Quennell, was just 17. What the books represented was not a generation, but a taste.

Finally, Marsh turned to address the issue of Modernism.

> Much admired modern work [he wrote] seems to me, in its lack of inspiration and its disregard of form, like gravy imitating lava. Its upholders may retort that much of the work which I prefer seems to

them, in its lack of inspiration and its comparative finish, like tapioca imitating pearls. Either view—possibly both—may be right. I will only say that with an occasional exception for some piece of rebelliousness or even levity which may have taken my fancy, I have tried to choose no verse but such as in Wordsworth's phrase

> The high and tender Muses shall accept
> With gracious smile, deliberately pleased.

And with that invocation of a great Georgian ancestor, *Georgian Poetry* came to an end—appropriately, one might say, in the year of the publication of two of the greatest Modernist texts: *The Waste Land* and *Ulysses*.

And was *Georgian Poetry* a good thing? The title certainly wasn't. To many people it seemed to make exhorbitant claims, both on the past and on the present. Marsh's obvious intention to claim kinship with the *other* Georgians of the Romantic Period struck Hardy, for instance, as lacking in 'the modesty of true genius' (he took the title to have been the poets' choice, which it wasn't); and the other implication, that an anthology called *Georgian Poetry* must represent the best poetry written in the reign of George V, seemed to some reviewers an absurdly inflated boast: the title, a TLS reviewer observed, 'sits like a man's hat on a boy's head . . .'

It is worth dwelling on this matter of the title, because it affected literary history. By imposing on his poets a collective label that they didn't deserve (and hadn't asked for), Marsh had made his sovereign's name virtually useless for ordinary historical purposes (in the senses in which we find it useful to talk about *Victorian* and *Edwardian*). Though of course history also contributed to the annihilation of the term, by dividing George's reign into parts—pre-war, post-war, Depression—that seem to have little to do with each other. The years from 1910 to 1936 have no collective characteristics that I can discern: there is no such thing as Georgian taste or Georgian architecture, no Georgian sensibility and no Georgian turn of mind. The term has no currency whatever, applied to the *reign*: all it means is 'the kind of poetry that Eddy Marsh fancied' (as in Pound's faint praise for a poem by Nancy Cunard: 'It is not Georgian, at least that is a gain').

But I think the anthologies were unfortunate quite apart from their titles. By bringing these poets together Marsh drew attention to their resemblances, and minimised their differences of poetic manner, and perhaps also of quality. Furthermore, he implied that they were a new school, something fresh that was happening in English poetry. And, by ceasing publication in 1922, he seemed to suggest that the kind of poetry that *Georgian Poetry* represented had come to an end—which was hard on poets like Drinkwater and Davies and de la Mare, who went on writing vigorously long after. One must acknowledge Marsh's generosity and dedication to the art and artists he believed in; but having said that, one must conclude that his influence on English literary history was disastrous.

If there had been no Edward Marsh, and no *Georgian Poetry*, how would we think of the Georgians? In one of two ways, I think. We might consider them, and others who were like them but didn't get into the anthologies, as representing a literary history that might have happened, but didn't—as the direction that English poetry might have taken if there had been no War, no lost audience, and no destruction of nature. They then become a literary lost battalion, a casualty of War and Modernism. The trouble with this account is that it assumes that what these poets represented in English poetic history ended with them. But it didn't any more than it began with them. The War may have deprived them of a base in society, may have created a literary climate in which they seemed ludicrously out of date; but it didn't kill the poets, or the kind of poetry they wrote.

Suppose we take instead the *other* way, and think of them as representatives of a tradition—neither the best nor the worst of it, but a part of it. We could call that tradition Wordsworthian, or perhaps Romantic; but I think a more useful term for the twentieth century is Hardyan (or if that sounds odd, The Hardy Tradition). All of the Georgians, of both generations, admired Hardy, and were influenced by him. Abercrombie, Blunden and Lawrence all wrote books about him, Drinkwater and de la Mare and Gibson reviewed him admiringly, Graves and Sassoon paid discipular visits to Max Gate, the fourth volume of *Georgian Poetry* was dedicated to him. From him each younger poet learned what he could: not every lesson that Hardy had to teach (he was wiser and craftier than they were) but some important things—the continuing life of traditional lyric verse, the range of ordinary speech, the significances that still exist in country matters. The lessons that they *didn't* learn were, I think, principally two: one was that if you continue to write in traditional metres, you must endlessly re-construct them; the Georgians were on the whole too easily content with habitual forms and cadences—Hardy wasn't. And more importantly, they missed the central point of Hardy's verse: that even in these traditional-sounding poems, the subject is *change*—that in the Post-Darwinian world, change is *always* the subject. And not learning that lesson, they were inclined to arrive at securities too easily.

One advantage of thinking of poets like Abercrombie and Drinkwater and Davies and Graves in the context of the Hardy tradition is that one can then add some important contemporaries to their ranks —poets who belong with them, but were never in *Georgian Poetry*: Edward Thomas, for instance, and Robert Frost, whom I would call the best of the Georgian Poets, if I were to use that misleading term at all.

Another advantage is that, once free of the collective and pejorative label of *Georgian*, some of these poets might get more serious attention. Harold Monro, for one—that strange, bitter man, who more than any other of the Georgian regulars found a style and a vision of his own. He was especially attuned to the non-human—not the birds and trees of easy Romanticism, but things like kettles and pots. He had an odd, harsh, truth-telling talent, I think (so did Eliot, who praised him in an obituary notice). And Davies—relentlessly naive, and less interested in form than any other readable poet I can think of, but with a unique and sometimes lovely gift. And Brooke: perhaps even he could be rehabilitated, separated from his war-sonnets, and seen as the only poet of the lot with an ironic sense (a true son of Hardy in that). And Blunden, who came in at the end, and survived as the last Georgian sensibility, but was a true country poet, and a good one.

Once one sees these poets in a living tradition, one can connect them not only backward to Hardy, and behind him to Wordsworth and Clare, but forward, to later poets like Andrew Young, R. S. Thomas, Cecil Day-Lewis, Geoffrey Grigson, and Philip Larkin. I'm not sure that any of these would be pleased to be linked back to the Georgians (though they'd like the Hardy connection well enough). But then it's not my task to please them. The fact remains that they are in the same persistent English tradition.

'You're not going to say,' my friend asked, 'that the Poundian revolution was all a mistake, are you?' No: as I've said, it wasn't a revolution. Revolutions destroy and replace. But twentieth-century modernism didn't do that: it simply added to the possibilities of poetry. It offered a new *kind* of poetry—disjunctive, international, non-discursive, symbolist—the formal expression of that sense of the death of civilisation that had come with the War. But the other tradition—quieter, English, familiar, ordinary—went on. And still goes on.

The Georgian poets are a link in the chain of that tradition. Not the most glorious link, but not negligible either. And a chain needs all of its links—that's what good literary history is all about.

THE HAUNTED BOOKS OF GEORGE GISSING

GILLIAN TRINDALL FRSL

Read 20th October 1983:
Colin Thubron, FRSL, in the Chair

TWO years ago, when giving this Carlos Coloma lecture, under the title 'The Art of Biography' Julian Symons indicated that you can't tell *the* truth about a person in a biography, however long and diligent: you can, he said, only tell *a* truth. If that dictum is valid for a whole book, then how much more valid it must be for a brief talk? I shall not therefore be attempting to tell you everything, or even all the important things, about Gissing's life, or about his novels—and certainly not about both in combination. It is, however, the combination which particularly interests me, and what I shall try to do now is to examine some themes in his work which I regard as particularly significant or interesting, and to look at the relation they may bear to his life.

First, I think, it is useful to place him in time, since he was in certain respects—though not all—very much a creature of his time. He was born in 1857, and died of lung disease in 1903 at the age of forty-six. He was therefore essentially a Victorian in experience and outlook. Unlike his near contemporaries Wells, Bennett and Hardy, he did not live on into the twentieth century to see the great material and social changes it would bring. He did not live to see the First World War (though he predicted it); still less did he live to inhabit the new mental and literary landscapes constructed by such innovators as D. H.

Lawrence, Lytton Strachey and Freud. In spite of a certain indi-
vidualism, and an admirable tendency to question the harsher and
more rigid conventions of his era, his personal mores were nevertheless basically those of the 19th century, and at that sometimes those of
the mid-century rather than those of the final decades through which
he actually lived. In his contradictory and conflict-ridden personality
there was a strong element of the nostalgic, of the natural conservative. In many respects, when he began to write, his perceived
landscape was that of Dickens—who had been his Favourite Author
during his passionately bookish childhood. He first lived in London as
a very young man at the end of the '70s—a period that he himself was
later to realise to have been 'the end of an epoch'. Years later, too, he
recorded this about his experience:

> . . . what I chiefly thought of was that now at length I could go
> hither and thither in London's immensity, seeking for the places
> which had been known to me by Dickens . . . making real to my
> vision what hitherto had been but names and insubstantial shapes
> . . . Thus, one day in the City, I found myself at the entrance to
> Bevis Marks! I had been making an application in reply to some
> advertisement—of course, fruitlessly; but what was that dis-
> appointment compared with the discovery of Bevis Marks! Here
> dwelt Mr Brass and Sally, and the Marchionness. Up and down that
> little street, this side and that, I went gazing and dreaming. No
> press of busy folk disturbed me; the place was quiet; it looked no
> doubt, much the same as when Dickens knew it. I am not sure I had
> any dinner that day, but, if not, I dare say I did not mind very
> much. (*The Immortal Dickens: Prefaces*)

This passage is, incidentally, typical of Gissing in a number of ways.
There is the oblique reference to poverty—'I'm not sure I had any
dinner that day'—and the slightly self-regarding suggestion that
books mattered to him more than food. This is Gissing playing
Starving Artist, a role which he only played for a brief while in reality,
but which affected his view of himself for the rest of his life. But the
main point is that this passage on Dickens' London is essentially a
literary view, both of London and of himself. In it, London is regarded
as fulfilling a literary stereotype for Gissing and Gissing himself is
fulfilling a literary stereotype for the reader.

This persistent Gissing-tendency has been called 'the view from the
British Museum Reading Room' and with a certain aptness. In *New*

Grub Street (1891), by general consensus his best, most integrated and original novel, the BM Reading Room does indeed figure as a nucleus from which almost all the relationships in the book, and most of the events good and bad, radiate. There the characters' paths cross, there personal emotions are involved, there is done much of the work that either illuminates the characters' lives or weighs them down intolerably—'. . . all those people about her' [one of them reflects] 'What aim had they save to make new books out of those already existing, that yet newer books might in turn be made out of theirs? This huge library, growing into unwieldiness, threatening to become a trackless desert of print—how intolerably it weighed upon the spirit . . . The fog grew thicker; she looked up at the windows beneath the dome and saw that they were a dusky yellow. Then her eye discerned an official walking along the upper gallery, and in pursuance of her grotesque humour, her mocking misery, she likened him to a black, lost soul doomed to wander in an eternity of vain research along endless shelves. Or again, the readers who sat here at these radiating lines of desks, what were they but hapless flies caught in a huge web, its nucleus the great circle of the Catalogue?'

There is a persistent, never-fully-expressed hint, in this absorbing and highly personal novel, of an almost revolutionary theory of Literature-as-Commodity, with the unfortunate writer as a slave to its production—a view bizarrely in keeping with the main motive-power of Victorian England although altogether at variance with Gissing's own more consciously conceived and expressed concepts: never was there, in fact, a more pre-industrial person than Gissing the writer, toiling away in his own room, counting neither hours nor effort, outside any social structure. More obviously, if simplistically, one might say that *New Grub Street* is an anti-novel novel, a book about how awful it is having to write books. The supreme irony is that the one strictly useful thing to come out of the British Museum Reading Room in the course of the novel is the recipe for poison which Biffen—a failed novelist—looks up there. He goes out to buy the ingredients from several different chemists and finally kills himself on Putney Common.

Walter Allen has said that one might imagine, reading Gissing's novels, that 'the sole end of life was that men and women should read together'. Even more accurate, I think, would be to say that Gissing's vision was that the man should read while the woman listened! Certainly the man-reading-aloud-to-the-woman situation crops up regularly in his books, perhaps as a kind of literary surrogate for love-making. (In those days of the three-volume novel and the rule of the lending libraries, the amount of material that an author could only hope to express obliquely or in code was of course enormously greater than in our own prosaic times.) But it is also true that, as far as we can tell, Gissing did read aloud—or attempt to read aloud—to all three of his wives. It seems to have been a constant item in his life as well as his fictions.

I say 'three wives'. In fact he was technically married to only two of them, but the third, who must be ranked as a common law wife, was relatively the most satisfactory of them—and certainly the only one with whom the reading aloud met with much success. The first was a young prostitute called Nell, whom he met while a student at Manchester. The second, Edith, whom he married twelve years later, after Nell's death, was respectable but hardly more suitable: she was a working class girl, stigmatised by one of Gissing's men friends as 'just a female'. The third, Gabrielle Fleury, whom he could not actually marry because Edith was still living, was a middle class French woman, somewhat consciously refined and cultured.

I have said that Gissing, in his way of viewing the world and dealing with it, tended to work from literature back to life rather than the other way round. The phenomenon is not unknown in highly literate people: it usually causes much misperception and consequent trouble, and Gissing was no exception to this. In addition, it seems to have made him curiously imperceptive where experience was on offer without so to speak, a literary antecedent to make it comprehensible to him. For instance, since he grew up in the northern industrial town of Wakefield, one might reasonably expect this to figure as a seminal influence in his work—but far from it. Unlike Arnold Bennett, who emerged from a similar lower middle class background at the same period in the Potteries, unlike Mrs Gaskell who was planted in Manchester by her husband's work and put the experience to good use, Gissing simply does not seem to have *seen* Wakefield as anything more than a place from which to escape. ('If any Dunfield schoolboy exhibited faculties of a kind uncommon in the town, he was despatched to begin life on a more promising scene; those who remained, who became the new generation of town councillors, of independent electors, were such as could not by any possibility have made a living elsewhere. Those elders who knew Dunfield best could not point to a single youth of fair endowments who looked forward to remaining in his native place.' (*A Life's Morning*, 1888.) It is, incidentally, interesting to speculate whether, had Gissing read Mrs Gaskell's novels in youth—which chronologically he could well have done—he would have seen towns like Wakefield in a different, more positive and literary light. But he was apparently only introduced to Mrs Gaskell's work fairly late in life, when the world of his boyhood was long behind him. As it is, the only novel in which Wakefield figures at all, even in a negative light, is *A Life's Morning*, and in order to write it he actually had to ask his brother Alfred, by letter, what was 'the nature' of the big mills in Wakefield. He seems not even to have realised that they were textile mills!

This tells one something not only about Gissing's personality but also about his upbringing. The latter was, indeed, remarkably segregated and more than a little odd. Gissing was the eldest son of a chemist with slender means, several other children, and literary and scientific aspirations. As such, the family lived very much in a social compartment of their own, educationally and culturally several cuts above the ordinary run of Wakefield trades-people, yet excluded almost entirely from the professional middle class society of the local lawyers, clergy, mill-owners and the like. Because of his evident intellectual gifts, and because his father's premature death made influential acquaintances rally round, young George made his way as a scholar, receiving eventually the sort of classical education that, at the period, was the mark of a gentleman. In spite of the doors this opened to him, it set him further apart in a category of his own; socially he became, and remained, something of a displaced person. H. G. Wells, who was his near-contemporary and later friend, and who had himself come from a similar shop-keeping background but without the equivocal benefit of a gentleman's education, was always rather uncomplimentary about both Gissing's scholarship and the value Gissing himself placed upon it: 'At the back of my mind I thought him horribly mis-educated', he once wrote, and went on to describe the Latin and Greek Gissing so prized as 'a vast collection of monumental masonry, a pale cemetery in the twilight, through which new conceptions hurry apologetically on their way to town finding neither home nor sustenance there.' (*Experiment in Autobiography*).

By the age of barely eighteen, Gissing had earned himself a scholarship to Owens College (which later became Manchester University). In the normal course of events, this gifted boy might have expected that a first degree here would be followed by a further award which would carry him to Oxford or Cambridge, and that eventually, by a series of natural developments, he would become a Fellow of one of those universities—a don. Fate, however, decided otherwise. (Or else Gissing himself, at the deepest level, had an obscure need to sabotage his own success and the security it might have brought him.) In Manchester, he met and fell in love with a girl who was either a prostitute or something very like it. In order to rescue her from ruin and set her up as a seamstress (such at any rate was his version of events) he took to stealing money from the college cloakroom. He was suspected, a trap was set and he was caught: the consequences were of a devastating harshness unthinkable today, when the adolescent perpetrator of such a minor crime would simply be shuffled off to the University Psychological Service. He was brought before the Justices and sentenced to *one month's* prison with hard labour. And, as a matter of course, he was dismissed from the college. The precise effect this retribution had on him, we will never know. All that can be said with certainty is that the pain and shame of it went so deep that it never even surfaced in his novels, right to the end of his life. One of two characters in his novels *do* go to prison or the like—on an unjust accusation—but we never actually follow them there. Evidently the whole episode, combined as it was with the terrible grief of losing face before his admiring family, became an unbearable no-go area of memory for him.

What is striking, of course, is that in the explanation he gave for his thefts life was in itself imitating art. It is surely significant that Murger and de Musset, both of whom depict the sexually promiscuous *midinette* as a romantic figure rather than a squalid one, were the favourite authors of his adolescence. It was his great misfortune that he was attempting to live out his literary dreams not in a Parisian attic but under the less forgiving roofs of bourgeois Manchester. But even so, the dream of 'saving' a victimised girl from ruin was a favourite British dream of the nineteenth century—see Hazlitt and de Quincy (and Gladstone!), see too Rossetti and his various versions of the *genre* painting *Found*, all of which depict a once-ruined country girl being rediscovered in the streets by her faithful, bucolic lover of ten years back. In a broader sense also, the 'rescue into love' (as Barbara Hardy has called it) was a common theme in Victorian literature. This, then, was the rich compost in which Gissing's fatally romantic and unrealistic attitude took root and grew. (He seems to have expected the Court to take a more lenient view when they heard of his good intentions, but unfortunately his revelations about Nell have produced the reverse effect).

Essentially, Gissing's error seems to have consisted in a confusion between sex and love—or, more precisely, between desire and the desire *to do good*. Throughout his novels and his life, these two strands of feeling appear to have been fatally intertwined. They surface particularly clearly in what came to be called his 'low life' novels —such as *Thyrza* and *The Nether World*.

One may fairly say that the disaster in Manchester broke Gissing's life: he certainly regarded it in that light. But one should also add that, looked at from another point of view, it was a blessing in disguise. There is no doubt that, had he gone on to lead the life of a celibate don he would have been both unhappy and frustrated and that his considerable potential as a novelist would probably have gone untapped. Those who have read his half-dozen best novels will appreciate that he was a born writer, and moreover one who (in spite of what he himself believed) worked best under pressure. The 'ideal conditions' of rural tranquillity, of which he believed himself to be chronically in need, in practice never produced his best work. His life was a series of repetitive attempts to 'free' himself—to avoid obligations, society, things that enroached upon his time for writing and each of these attempts brought in train a loneliness, isolation and depression that in fact were counter-productive. He seems to have been worse than most writers are at knowing what was actually *good* for him, either as a writer or as a man. Both his best novels, *New Grub Street* and *The Odd Women* (1893) were in fact written in brief spaces of time, under great pressure, while a lot else was going on in his life. While *The Odd Women* was in process he actually had to stop at intervals to prepare feeds for his new-born son!

But I am anticipating. To return to his early years—with lemming-like persistence he insisted on fitting reality to the romantic idyll by marrying Manchester Nell. The consequences were as his family and friends could have predicted and no doubt did. Nell was a hopelessly incompetent wife by anyone's standards, let alone those of the basically fastidious and sensitive Gissing. She drank, she took up with other men: the whole thing was impossible. You can read all about it in his first novel, *Workers in the Dawn* (1879)—if, that is, you can find a copy: neither the British Museum nor the London Library possess it. But it would be a mistake to imagine that *Workers in the Dawn* depicts what had happened already when Gissing was writing. On the contrary, the book was published just *before* he actually married Nell and is an all-too-accurate evocation of what Gissing was afraid might come to pass and what indeed, two or three years later, did. This is the first example, but by no means the last, of Gissing trying out, as it were, in fiction, a course of action that is traceable *subsequently* in his work. He was to do this in *New Grub Street*, in a more elaborate form, and again in *In The Year of Jubilee* (1894). In both instances, he also went ahead and made the very mistakes in life, or similar ones, which he had already predicted for an alter ego in a novel. It was as if the writer Gissing knew more than the man, and the man was unable to make use of this knowledge. He was not unique among writers in this—I suspect, indeed, the phenomenon is more common than is often realised—but he does present a particularly clear and disconcerting example of it.

I have already mentioned the theme of altruism, the desire to do good. This desire seems to have been personally strong in Gissing; his family and friends remarked that it was one of the brightest aspects of a personality that was, in certain respects, flawed and sombre. His early books, too, are full of a rather ingenuous, wish-fulfilment working out of theme: the characters have a marked tendency to give away overcoats to poor old men, or baked potatoes to hungry street boys, or—with a certain advance in thought—to join radical movements for the betterment of the labouring classes. Gissing indeed went in for this himself in his early days, but later his inbred élitism and conservatism seems to have turned him away from the company into which such interests led him. He was indeed the most curious mixture of democrat and snob, and his naturally polemic tendency—his constitutional inability to regard any matter dispassionately—made him ever-liable to reject with contumely the very cause he had earlier espoused with enthusiasm. By 1888 he was castigating William Morris himself for associating with the working classes and maintaining that a writer must 'keep apart' to preserve his integrity. But he continued nevertheless to take an emotional and intellectual interest in the theme of altruism. It crops up interesting in *Demos* (1886) in a study of a self-made working class entrepreneur that is astute but not kind, and reappears later in more sophisticated form in *Our Friend the Charlatan* (1901) with a cynical reappraisal of the roots of philanthropy.

But inevitably there was another element in his sympathy towards the working classes and his subsequent fear of them. Wells, that kind, concerned but basically disloyal friend, wrote after Gissing's death that Gissing had been 'terribly obsessed by the sexual question'. Indeed one may reasonably conclude that the theme of loneliness that crops up so frequently in his novels is something more than an accurate reflection of his isolated life: it also probably serves as a literary code for that more specifically sexual frustration that could not possibly be discussed overtly in a nineteenth century English novel. The nearest Gissing came to an admission on this matter was in his diary, in which he wrote abruptly, amid much mundane stuff, 'I shall never do any good work till I am married'. A few months later he did marry—Edith Underwood, that working class 'female', whom his acquaintances all regarded as an inexplicable choice for this bookish, highly-strung man.

For the ostensible reason for the marriage we need to look to *New Grub Street* (1891). The premise behind the persistent failed-marriage theme in this novel is that, because of the precariousness of his financial position, no man of letters or writer can realistically contemplate marriage with a girl of good family. In support and elaboration of this, the novel offers two sample marriages, that of man-of-letters Alfred Yule with a working class wife and that of novelist Edwin Reardon with the middle class Amy. Now *New Grub Street* was written, at great pressure and after several false starts, while Gissing was actually courting Edith: it was therefore as if he were trying out life in literature in a two-fold way. On the one hand the Yule marriage can hardly be regarded as successful, but this may all be ascribed to Alfred Yule's irascible temper; the novel allows one to believe that a gentler, kinder man of culture would have been able to live in modest contentment with so pliable and submissive a wife, and so Gissing may have persuaded himself. On the other hand the Reardon marriage is a more careful and sophisticated study in fundamental incompatibility: Amy has married Edwin under the impression that she is becoming the wife of someone who will shortly be a great man; it is the supposed identity of 'writer' that attracts her, not the lonely realities of a writer's life. When she realises that her husband, far from being a celebrity is heading, after a promising start, for obscurity and failure, her consternation is great: '. . . in the grief of her disappointment she would rather have had him flare into worthless popularity than flicker down into total extinction, which it almost seemed was to be his fate. She knew so well how "people" were talking of him and her.' Money is also (of course) running out: 'Presently she would become an object of pity; there would be talk of "poor Mrs Reardon". It was intolerable.'

I might add in passing that the menace of 'total extinction' is of course not just Amy's problem. It is the quintessential writer's problem, and I shall return to it.

But why, the question immediately presents itself, did Gissing have to work so hard to convince himself that marriage with a middle class girl was indeed out of the question? Not all middle class girls were philistine, ambitious Amys, and this he really knew. Late-Victorian society indeed was full of superfluous girls of genteel birth longing to marry on almost any terms and frequently failing to do so. Gissing's own two sisters were broadly in this category; so were other women to whom both Wells and his friend Morley Roberts hopefully introduced him, but with his writer's mind he knew it anyway. In *The Odd Women*—the title itself tells much—a naive man asks a worldly woman friend ' "Do you seriously tell me . . . that there are ladies in good society who would have married me just because I have a few hundred a year?" ' The woman replies: ' "My dear boy, I would get together a round dozen in two or three days. Girls who would make good, faithful wives, in mere gratitude to the man who saved them from—horrors." ' (This novel, incidentally, also contains a perfect example—the Widdowson marriage—of the folly of casting someone in life in an inappropriate role; the very thing of which Gissing himself was so frequently, in his romantic relations, culpable.)

In short, with one part of his mind Gissing understood how society functioned. He was in many ways an acute social observer. So, why again, why did he not seek out in life some vicar's daughter, governess or valiant music teacher as accustomed to financial insecurity as himself? Why, in short, Edith? who, as it was to turn out, was not even pliable and submissive, but ill-tempered to the point of unbalance.

It is here that I introduce—hardly with a fanfare, perhaps rather with the Dead March from Saul—the all-important Guilty Secret theme in Gissing's life and work. In his novels, hero after hero is mysteriously unworthy to approach women of suitable class and education with offers of matrimony. Time after time, the Gissing alter ego is deterred by—well, by what? Sometimes it is a humble background, anxiously dissembled. Frequently it is lack of money. But often again it is something more eccentric: a previous secret marriage (twice); a shabby motive for altruism, the adoption of a lofty pose for material gain (see *Born in Exile*) or some other fatal dishonesty. Sometimes this involves a vague but pervasive suggestion of male nastiness, the then almost inevitable consequence of what today would be called the double-standard. As one of the characters says in *The Crown of Life* (1899) 'There is nothing bad to know about women.' Therefore, in the terms by which that society lived, there *must* be something bad to know about rather a lot of men.

But the point I wish to make is that always, in novel after novel, the professed explanation for the hero's inability to marry suitably is made to bear too much weight in rational terms. Somewhere along the line, each time, plot and emotion part company. In *Born in Exile* (1892) for instance, Godwin Peak's guilty secret is that he pretends to a religious faith he does not feel in order to take Holy Orders in the interests of social advancement—something, incidentally, which Gissing himself might well have found himself doing had he pursued his originally destined career in university circles, since most dons were at that time still in Orders. But the interesting thing is that Godwin Peak *behaves* like a guilty man in the book quite a long time before he starts this specific subterfuge. Or, as Middleton Murry said, looking at the several novels in which lack of money on which to propose marriage is the presenting reason: 'What is peculiar about his heroes is that they are frustrated by something more—and less visible—than their poverty.'

What then is this substantial but invisible inhibition? Several possibilities obviously present themselves. I have already said that Gissing's traumatic experience of prosecution and prison affected him at so deep a level that he was unable even to make use of it in his work: arguably, a lifelong fear that respectable friends would find out about this early disaster affected all his relationships, and this chronic fear of some unnamed exposure transferred itself, appropriately or inappropriately, to almost all his central characters. In addition, there has been a persistent suggestion—for which I believe the late and gossipy Frank Swinnerton to have been responsible—that Gissing contracted VD from Nell, and that it was essentially this dreadful knowledge that made him incapable of approaching a 'nice' woman for marriage.

I am dubious of this, for two reasons. In the first place, Gissing, whatever else he was, was no cad, and if he had been unable to approach a middle class girl for this reason would have felt himself equally unable to approach a respectable working class one. There is, to be sure, a certain amount of evidence that he himself *thought*, at one stage, he might be carrying syphilis, but in this he was (once again!)

following a prevailing literary convention: syphilis was the great veiled bogey of the nineteenth century writer, the dark side of romanticism. But he was apparently reassured on this point by a doctor friend; at all events he not only married Edith and fathered two children but later, towards the end of the century, set off for a new life in France with Gabrielle Fleury, a step he certainly would not have taken had he still been harbouring any real-life sense of contamination. It seems that, seeking the origin of the Guilty Secret in his works, we have to look not in his body or even in his mind, but rather into the irrational well of his emotions.

The occasional, faint mysterious references in his diary and letters to some 'taint' in himself, to which the avid Swinnerton gave a concrete interpretation, seem to me more suggestive of a reference to chronic and cyclic depression. Certainly there is ample circumstantial evidence that Gissing was a clinical depressive, and although, like so many depressives, he never really seems to have come to terms with the subjective and variable nature of his moods, he nevertheless does appear to have been intermittently aware that they were not wholly the product of external circumstances. There is a very interesting short story of his, *The Elixir*, published in the 1890s, about a man dogged by misfortune, reaching a state of despair, who is suddenly rescued by a magic change of luck. As a realistic story it is wholly implausible. But as a way of the writer saying in code 'If only I could rid my own personality of this flaw then everything would be different' it is a most revealing study.

What we seem to be seeing here, then, is a man with a deeper insecurity in him than poverty, insignificant background or even than a dubious past; it is, rather, the chronic, anxious insecurity of a man without a fixed identity. Wells wrote perceptively of Gissing 'He was terrified at the prospect of incompatibility. His sensitiveness to reactions made every relationship a pose, and he had no natural, customary *persona* for miscellaneous use.'

I would remark merely in closing that this is peculiarly a writer's insecurity. The writer's need to assume other's skins and empathise with their problems while yet standing apart from them . . . the essentially introspective, lonely occupation of literary creation . . . the perpetual dependence on ephemeral and easily damaged self-confidence . . . all these characteristics make the novelist chronically prone to a self-regarding doubt. Writing, after all, is essentially a confidence trick. Gissing spent far too much of his time for his own good as a writer—let alone for his comfort—thrown upon his own insubstantial resources. The material of *New Grub Street*, that agonising and detailed indictment of the writer's very existence, was not only all round him: it was also within him. It was not by chance that it was the only entirely integrated and successful book he ever wrote.

HARDY'S WESSEX

DESMOND HAWKINS OBE, FRSL

Read 14th April 1983:
Dr Robert Gittings, CBE, FRSL, in the Chair

IT'S surprising what you can learn from a telephone directory. I looked up 'Wessex' in mine and I found eighty-eight entries. Eighty-eight —ranging from Wessex Academy of English to Wessex World Travel Ltd. On top of that I'm obliged to make extravagant payments to the Wessex Water Authority, about which I can make futile complaints to the Member of the European Parliament who represents the Wessex constituency. In the naming of parts of England Thomas Hardy certainly did not labour in vain—because of course it was he who revived the title of the old Saxon kingdom and gave it its fresh modern currency.

When and why did he do it? He first used the word in *Far from the Madding Crowd* in 1874, and in a preface which he added later he gave this explanation:

It was in the chapters of *Far from the Madding Crowd*, as they appeared month by month in a popular magazine, that I first ventured to adopt the word 'Wessex' from the pages of early English history, and give it a fictitious significance as the existing name of the district once included in that extinct kingdom. The series of novels I projected being mainly of the kind called local, they seemed to require a territorial definition of some sort to lend unity to their scene. Finding that the area of a single county did not afford a canvas large enough for this purpose, and that there were objections to an invented name, I disinterred the old one.

Since then the appellation which I had thought to reserve to the horizons and landscapes of a partly real, partly dream-country, has become more and more popular as a practical provincial definition; and the dream-country has, by degrees, solidified into a utilitarian region which people can go to, take a house in, and write to the papers from.

I think there are two key-phrases in that explanation. One is 'a territorial definition of some sort to lend unity'. The other is 'a partly real, partly dream-country'. They indicate the values that Hardy found in this concept of 'Wessex' as he gradually developed it. He liked to live among the scenes he was describing, to draw directly from real living models, and yet not to be constrained by a mere verisimilitude. His west country towns and villages are authentic—often transparently so—but he reserves the right to transpose, enlarge, contract and rearrange to meet the particular requirements of the work in hand. The 'partly real' and the 'partly dream' must learn to accommodate each other.

The unity created in this way built up a gathering momentum from one book to the next and created an extra sort of copyright. Other writers could enter Dorchester and Stinsford but they could hardly set foot in Casterbridge and Mellstock. Hardy had, from necessity, an alert attention to the business side of authorship and he soon saw the advantage of having his books advertised as *Wessex* novels, not just as novels. In a letter urging one of his publishers to adopt this practice he wrote:

I find that the name *Wessex*, which I was the first to use in fiction, is getting to be taken up everywhere: and it would be a pity for us to lose the right to it for want of asserting it.

Here I should perhaps interject a brief description of Wessex for the benefit of those who are not already familiar with the territory that Hardy defined. He spoke of *six* counties though his own map shows seven. The six were Dorset, Somerset and Wiltshire—which represent the heartland of his Wessex—plus two more on the east, Berkshire and Hampshire, and one to the westward, Devon. Avon is irrelevant since it did not exist as a county in Hardy's lifetime. The seventh is Cornwall, which Hardy named in a rather ambiguous fashion as 'off-Wessex'—recognising its apartness from any Saxon tradition.

County boundaries are not particularly helpful. Berkshire includes Windsor, and Aldershot is in Hampshire, but neither place seems to owe any allegiance to Wessex. The scenes that Hardy made his own are the characteristic landscapes of the southwest peninsula—the rolling chalk downland and the clay vales, the sheer cliffs and little harbours of the western ocean, the barren heathland and the high moors. It is out of these that Hardy created the partly real, partly dream country which began as his birthright and which became the theatre of his imagination. The identities of counties started to fade as he redesigned Wessex in his own terms—Egdon Heath, The Vale of the Little Dairies, Wessex Heights and Lyonnesse. These are the newly minted Wessex of the poet's vision.

Looking back on his life Hardy wrote 'I am convinced that it is better for a writer to know a little bit of the world remarkably well than to know a great part of the world remarkably little.' The even-handed distribution of his fictitious place-names over the map of Wessex suggests that he knew this 'little bit of the world' *uniformly* well, which in turn invites the question of how he gained his knowledge. From Basingstoke to Penzance is something more than a day's march and Hardy's opportunities for extensive and leisurely travel were not great. It's true he was an enthusiastic cyclist but he did not acquire a bicycle—according to his latest biographer, Michael Millgate—until 1896, when all his novels were already written. In the thirty-five previous years of his adult life he had spent a sizeable part in London and had throughout been so preoccupied with the immediate task of earning a living as to have little leisure for touring.

His knowledge of Wessex was therefore in zones of greatly differing intensity. There was the closely encompassed world of his childhood and youth—the world of Stinsford and Puddletown, Dorchester and Weymouth, Egdon Heath and the Valley of the Great Dairies. Then there was the wider Dorset scene that opened from the homes of his married life—at Sturminster Newton, Swanage and Wimborne before he settled finally at Dorchester. Across the Dorset border the neighbouring areas of Somerset, Wiltshire and Hampshire came easily enough within his physical range. Taken together these are the ingredients that make up what I spoke of as the *heartland* of Hardy's Wessex. If I had to identify its four corners I should draw one axis from Salisbury Plain to Lyme Bay, the other from the New Forest to 'sad Sedgemoor'.

With the outlying territories he was less familiar. Before he acquired his bicycle his only means of transport were those two other innovations of his lifetime—the steamboat and the railway. He saw the southern coastline of Wessex while travelling by sea from London to Plymouth and made other brief excursions from the Dorset ports and harbours which are reflected in his novels. The railway was a liberating force for a young man of his class and generation. I doubt if any major poet has written more poems depicting railway scenes than has Hardy. Even so he had only a slight and piecemeal acquaintance with Devon and Cornwall, apart from that one small sector near Boscastle to which I shall come later; and the northern part of Wessex in general belongs more perhaps to R. D. Blackmore and Richard Jefferies than to Hardy.

The novel in which he first introduced his concept of Wessex was his fourth publication. The three previous novels show a considerable uncertainty as to the way his talents might develop. The first is a melodrama; the second, in his own definition, is 'a rural painting of the Dutch School'; the third is a curious hybrid of tangled romance and black comedy. What is common to all three is the assumption that the Wessex natives, the rustic cottagers, are quaint, humorous and not to be treated with the same degree of seriousness as the gentry, the educated characters. In this attitude the young Hardy was simply following a well established tradition in which the agricultural labourer—the besmocked figure known contemptuously as Hodge—had no literary value except as a quaint buffoon.

On the evidence of those early novels Hardy seems to have fancied himself as a satirist, and it is a role he never entirely surrendered though he greatly refined his technique to the masterly ironies of his later work. But at the outset he addressed himself to satire at two levels—a sharp and biting satire of society at large, and a gentler teasing satire on the village worthies of his home background. Ben Jonson and the Restoration wits provided his models for giving to some of his characters the names of William Worm, Mrs Menlove, Mr Ladywell and Miss Vashti Sniff. And in his bid to amuse the reading public with the quainter features of Dorset he parodied its village names with such inventions as Tantrum Clangley and Puddle-sub-Mixen—villages which you won't find in the ultimate, official Wessex, but you will find in his earlier novels.

In the preface he wrote in 1912 to *Under the Greenwood Tree* Hardy commented that the realities out of which his story was spun 'were material for another kind of study of this little group of church musicians than is found in the chapters here penned so lightly, even so farcically and flippantly at times. But circumstances would have rendered any aim at a deeper, more essential, more transcendent handling unadvisable at the date of writing.'

In plain words he had to consider his market, as a beginner; and he had to find his own way forward by trial and error. The significance of *Far from the Madding Crowd* with its inception of Wessex was that it established the idiom in which he could achieve that 'deeper, more essential, more transcendent handling'. Where his first impulse had been to detach himself from his native background, to stand off at the distance that satire requires, he now began to ally himself with his contemporaries' absorption in the subjects of regional identity, dialect, survivals of folk-lore and legend, and anything that could be recognised as a distinctively local flavour in a landscape and its inhabitants.

The characteristic thrust of the classical writers of the eighteenth century had been in quite a different mode—towards a uniformity of culture, a standardised elegance and precision expressed in national norms of language and social behaviour and aesthetic taste. The prevailing atmosphere had favoured the compiling of dictionaries and codes of etiquette, leaving no doubt of the rules of right and wrong. The civilised society was then seen as an enclave, centred on the capital city, and excluding those other and lower forms of life beyond the pale which were no fit subject for a serious mind to contemplate, except in jocular buffooneries.

What this stabilising culture of the eighteenth century was ultimately incapable of resisting was the incoming tide of new ideas that we now identify with Walter Scott and the Lake poets and the whole Romantic Movement in Europe which came to dominate the nineteenth century with its emotional excesses, its cultivation of morbidity and horror, its antiquarian pursuits and Gothic enthusiasms, its intellectual radicalism and its exaltation of the spirit of place. At several levels Hardy's immediate predecessors and contemporaries undertook what might be described as a national stocktaking, turning out neglected mediaeval cupboards and confronting familiar landscapes with a fresh set of questions.

I mentioned the new importance given to a distinctively local flavour in a landscape and its inhabitants. As an example of such a flavour let me assemble one or two of Hardy's descriptive passages about Egdon Heath:

> that ancient country whose surface never had been stirred to a finger's depth, save by the scratching of rabbits, since brushed by the feet of the earliest tribes . . .

> To many persons this Egdon was a place which had slipped out of its century generations ago, to intrude as an uncouth object into this . . .

> Civilisation was its enemy.

The tone of voice makes it clear that Hardy was not its enemy. For him its uncouth wildness hallowed it as the spiritual home of the rebel and the outcast. In *The Mayor of Casterbridge* it was to Egdon Heath that Henchard went to die.

It is a mark of the stature of a writer that he responds to the deepest forces that are moulding his generation and that he adds something of himself to those forces—some new direction or increased momentum. I think I can demonstrate this in Hardy's case by two more descriptions of Egdon Heath—one written about seventy years before his birth, the other about fifty years after his death. I take the first from John Hutchins's *History and Antiquities of the County of Dorset*:

> Near Piddletown begins a large tract of heathy ground, which from thence eastwards occupies a great part of the southern coast, and extends to Hampshire and Surrey . . . This is professedly the most barren part of the county; and Nature, who has in other parts distributed her beauties with so liberal a hand, seems here, by way of contrast, to exhibit a view of all others the most dreary and unpleasing.

That is how Egdon Heath appeared to the eye of a beholder in the 1770s. By contrast an article in *The Times* last year by Christopher Booker spoke of it in these words—'this strange and unique fragment of Britain's landscape is as irreplaceable as a Gothic cathedral'—and he went on to argue that it should be just as zealously preserved.

What a contrast! What a revolution in taste!

It would be oversimplifying the difference between the two writers to ascribe it solely to the fact that Hutchins was denied the opportunity, which Booker has evidently enjoyed, of reading *The Return of the Native*; but the germ of truth is there. If Hutchins spoke with the voice of Pope and the Age of Reason, it is the tones of Wordsworth and the Romantic Movement that we recognise in Hardy's appreciation of wilderness values, of the pristine and undomesticated scene.

In the preface he wrote to the fifth edition of *Tess of the d'Urbervilles*, in 1892, Hardy made the point that public attitudes may be subtly influenced to take a new direction as the result, not of overt argument, but of 'sentiment' expressed in a novel. In the immediate case of *Tess* it was in the area of social morality, and more specifically of sexual morality, that the novel was influential; but the same principle could be applied to *The Return of the Native* in terms of landscape. The shift in values that Hardy's portrayal of Egdon Heath represented was formulated in the most challenging way in this passage:

> Haggard Egdon appealed to a subtler and scarcer instinct, to a more recently learnt emotion, than that which responds to the sort of beauty called charming and fair.
>
> Indeed, it is a question if the exclusive reign of this orthodox beauty is not approaching its last quarter . . . human souls may find themselves in closer and closer harmony with external things wearing a sombreness distasteful to our race when it was young. The time seems near, if it has not actually arrived, when the chastened sublimity of a moor, a sea, or a mountain will be all of nature that is absolutely in keeping with the moods of the more thinking among mankind.

To eighteenth century eyes the barren heath had been a challenge and its continued existence almost a moral reproach. Arthur Young's comment on Egdon was characteristic—'What fortunes are here to be made by spirited improvers!' The new aesthetic that Hardy introduced was as revolutionary in its way as the paintings of Turner.

I must not dwell on Egdon Heath for too long or exclusively. What Hardy displays in Wessex is a variety of landscapes—each with its distinctive nature; and as he paints the scene he emphasises its mutual relationship with the human protagonists so that they are not merely figures in a landscape but are part of the landscape. When Tess first arrives in the Valley of the Great Dairies in a hopeful mood it is 'on a thyme-scented, bird-hatching morning in May' and the waters of the river Froom 'were clear as the pure River of Life shown to the Evangelist, rapid as the shadow of a cloud, with pebbly shallows that prattled to the sky all day long'. It was a scene that 'sent her spirits up wonderfully . . . She heard a pleasant voice in every breeze, and in every bird's note seemed to lurk a joy'. And as summer approaches her love for Angel Clare and the flowering of Nature seem to mature in step with each other. The stirring sexuality of the girl is in harmony with what Hardy calls 'the leafy time when arborescence seems to be the one thing aimed at out of doors . . . Rays from the sunrise drew forth the buds and stretched them into long stalks, lifted up sap in noiseless streams, opened petals, and sucked out scents in invisible jets and breathings.'

In the Blackmore Vale, the Vale of the Little Dairies, the tone and mood are different again. The heavy clay land, where in Hardy's phrase 'the fields are never brown and the springs never dry', softens into scenes of mist and a blue haze in which ancient customs and superstitions flourish. Hardy made the point explicitly, asserting that 'Superstitions linger longest on these heavy soils.' In *The Woodlanders* the conversation of foresters and woodmen turns to 'the mysterious sights they had seen—only to be accounted for by supernatural agency; of white witches and black witches.' Marty South's father is convinced of the active malevolence of a particular tree which he believes is intending to enslave and ultimately destroy him. When the tree is felled he dies. On Midsummer Eve the village girls go into the woodlands to perform an act of magic which will reveal their future husbands. And Tess's mother (at Marlott) is so convinced of the potency of her volume of *The Compleat Fortune-Teller* that she will not let it remain in the house at night but has it lodged in the thatch of an outhouse—a beautifully observed detail in her portrayal.

I am moving more closely, as you will have gathered, to the associations that bind a landscape and its inhabitants together. Within the unity of Wessex Hardy's characters seem to grow up out of the land as naturally as its plants and trees. In them geology and climate are reinforced by tradition and history. In each of his major landscapes the human overtones are unmistakeable. As an example let me take the description of Norcombe Hill at the beginning of *Far from the Madding Crowd*. It is a night scene on the downland where Gabriel Oak grazes his sheep. Taken purely as a passage of descriptive prose it is masterly, culminating in the majestic sentence 'To persons standing alone on a hill during a clear midnight such as this, the roll of the world eastward is almost a palpable movement.'

But there is more to come when Hardy describes the hill itself:

Norcombe Hill . . . was one of the spots which suggest to a passerby that he is in the presence of a shape approaching the indestructible as nearly as any to be found on earth. It was a featureless convexity of chalk and soil—an ordinary specimen of those smoothly-outlined protuberances of the globe which may remain undisturbed on some great day of confusion, when far grander heights and dizzy granite precipices topple down.

There Hardy is drawing us into the deeper atmosphere of the story and the forces that will bear on the drama which begins to unfold. The epithets applied to Norcombe—'featureless' and 'ordinary'—are the concealing attributes of that staunch survivor Gabriel Oak, who is described as occupying 'morally the vast middle space of Laodicean neutrality' and as 'a man whose moral colour was a kind of pepper-and-salt mixture'. He embodies the unspectacular, undemonstrative virtues that Hardy liked to display in his Wessex heroes, in contrast with the impetuous passions and flashy, wayward impulses of Gab-riel's rivals—Sergeant Troy and Mr Boldwood. It is Troy and Bold-wood who are represented in the grander heights and dizzy precipices which will eventually topple down. It is Gabriel Oak who persists as a virtually indestructible Norcombe Hill among the Alps of treachery and the Himalayas of hatred.

Nothing could demonstrate more clearly the fact that these land-scapes of Hardy's are not idly pretty sequences of fine writing but theatres of his imagination in which character and background rein-force each other. They embody the comment he made on Turner's water-colours—'each is a landscape *plus* a man's soul'. And in the light of that he set himself the task 'to see the deeper reality underlying the scenic.'

In 1875, after reading *Lorna Doone*, Hardy addressed to its author, R. D. Blackmore, a letter of appreciation from which I quote these extracts:

I have just read your finest book (as I think)—Lorna Doone, and I cannot help writing just one line to tell you how astonished I was to find what it contained . . . Little phases of nature which I thought nobody had noticed but myself were continually turning up in your book. A kindred sentiment between us in so many things is, I suppose, partly because we both spring from the West of England.

This tribute to Blackmore indicates that, like William Barnes, he was a pioneer in the creation of a 'West of England' consciousness, opening up the new literary territory that Hardy was eventually to dominate. It is interesting to notice the convergence of Blackmore's celebrated hero, the Exmoor yeoman, Jan Ridd, with Hardy's shepherd Gabriel Oak and the forester and hurdle-maker, Giles Winterborne, in *The Woodlanders*, and Diggory Venn the reddle-man in *The Return of the Native*—all of them sturdy and self-reliant, shy and emotionally controlled and restrained. These were new hero-figures, with their strong regional characteristics. And they highlight the general trend of Hardy's development of the native elements of Wessex.

He was at first inclined to reserve much of the centre of his stage in the conventional way for the gentry, for heiresses and landowners, professional people such as country parsons and suspiciously auto-biographical young architects—characters whose allegiance was to a city culture with its outposts in manor-house and rectory. Gradually Hardy tipped the balance towards the vernacular elements, in such a way that it hardly seems fanciful to speak of Wessex as possessing—or re-possessing—him. Not only in his novels and short stories, but in his poems also, a host of hitherto neglected figures come before us—shepherd and dairymaid, carter and common soldier, hay-trusser and drover and many more such. From providing a back-ground of humour and homely comment they move to the centre of the stage and take over the leading roles.

There is an incident in one of his short stories—'The Waiting Supper', written in 1887 which illustrates this shift of focus. The scene is a rural christening-party. One of the guests, Squire Everard's daughter, Christine, is in conversation with Mr Bellston, a sophisti-cated young man from London, who remarks, 'It does one's heart good to see these simple peasants enjoying themselves'. To which Christine replies 'O Mr. Bellston! Don't be too sure about that word "simple"! You little think what they see and meditate! Their reason-ings and emotions are as complicated as ours.'

It was in the same year that Hardy completed *The Woodlanders*, in which he described the village of little Hintock as 'one of those sequestered spots outside the gates of the world where, . . . from time to time, dramas of a grandeur and unity truly Sophoclean are enacted in the real, by virtue of the concentrated passions and closely-knit interdependence of the lives therein'.

In the light of those two passages it is no wonder that the jauntily satirical sketches of the earlier novels are superseded by the major portraits of Marty South and Tess and Jude. Jude the *Obscure*—what a challenge that word must have been! Still is. It was as the spokesman for the obscure people of Wessex that Hardy found his destiny. It was they who filled his pages with so much animation and elemental passion.

The single figures of his Wessex heroes and heroines are presented to us in terms of tragedy, but they are accompanied by a murmuring vernacular chorus which retains a satirical sharpness and dry humour that are distinctively Hardy's own. Unlike Barnes and Blackmore he made no attempt at a literal phonetic rendering of dialect but he had a wonderful ear for the cadence and style of Wessex speech, which he represented with a minimum of verbal devices.

This rustic chorus he used in two ways. By its homeliness and primitive warmth it kept the higher flights of tragedy down to earth. It was a pledge of authenticity. You need only recall Marty South's elegy at the grave of Giles Winterborne to recognise that. And, at a different level, the freedom of comic expression in dialect was used by Hardy as a licence to say what would hardly have been acceptable in a serious manner. Let me remind you of that scene at the Buck's Head in *Far from the Madding Crowd* when Jan Coggan is comparing Church and Chapel:

' "I won't say much for myself; I don't wish to", Coggan continued . . . "But I've never changed a single doctrine; I've stuck like a plaster to the old faith I was born in. Yes; there's this to be said for the Church, a man can belong to the Church and bide in his cheerful old inn, and never trouble or worry his mind about doctrines at all. But to be a meetinger, you must go to chapel in all winds and weathers, and make yerself as frantic as a skit. Not but that chapel-members be clever chaps enough in their way. They can lift up beautiful prayers out of their own heads, all about their families and shipwrecks in the newspaper".

"Chapel-folk be more hand-in-glove with them above than we", said Joseph thoughtfully.

"Yes", said Coggan, "We know very well that if anybody do go to heaven, they will. They've worked hard for it, and they deserve to have it, such as 'tis. I bain't such a fool as to pretend that we who stick to the Church have the same chance as they, because we know we have not. But I hate a feller who'll change his old ancient doctrines for the sake of getting to heaven. I'd as soon turn King's evidence for the few pounds you get".'

It is in such speeches that you are likely to find the more mordant of Hardy's social comments. He was born in 1840 at Higher Bockhampton after a decade of unrest and violence in the surrounding villages, but you will look in vain for any account in his stories of the burning of ricks and smashing of machinery during the agricultural riots at Puddletown in 1830; or the arrest and trial of the so-called Martyrs of Tolpuddle in 1833. However, if you listen to the farm-labourers talking to the Scotsman, Farfrae, in the bar of the *Three Mariners* in *The Mayor of Casterbridge* you will be struck by the realism of Christopher Coney when he tells Farfrae—'we be bruckle folk here—the best o' us hardly honest sometimes, what with hard winters, and so many mouths to fill, and God-a'mighty sending his little taties so terrible small to fill 'em with'. And it is the spectre of transportation to a convict settlement which colours his rejection of Farfrae's sentimental patriotism, with the words—'For my part I've no more love for my country than I have for Botany Bay!'

It passes as rustic humour. Its undertones are unmistakeable.

I have kept back until last two Wessex landscapes that you would not expect me to overlook—Lyonnesse and Wessex Heights. Lyonnesse was the name Hardy gave to the coast of north Cornwall in the vicinity of Boscastle and Tintagel. 'Wessex Heights' is the title of a poem which celebrates the commanding downland crests and hill-tops which sound like a litany in Hardy's writings—'from Ingpen Beacon eastward to Wylls Neck westwardly'. Taken together Lyonnesse and Wessex Heights lead us to the more romantic and more personal fastnesses of Hardy's dream-world.

It was by the mere chance of his employment as an architectural draughtsman that Hardy first went to Cornwall, to prepare plans for the restoration of the church at St Juliot. Acting as his hostess at the rectory was the rector's sister-in-law, Emma Gifford, and this casual encounter had an electrifying effect on Hardy. He fell instantly in love with Emma and in due course married her. And he fell in love with the Cornish setting in which he found her. His 'West-of-Wessex girl', as he called her, introduced him to a world very different from 'Haggard Egdon' and the cautious ordinariness of Norcombe Hill. There was no trace of satire or irony in this land of legends outside the prosaic Saxon

kingdom where Hardy, like a latter-day Tristan, found—in his own
words—'an Yseult of my own'.

> She opened the door of the West to me,
>   With its loud sea-lashings,
>   And cliff-side clashings
> Of waters rife with revelry.

That is the first verse of one of his later poems, written after Emma's
death, and it continues 'She opened the door of Romance to me'. For
the rest of his life the wild Atlantic coast of the far West was to appeal
to all that was romantic in Hardy's temperament. 'Lyonnesse' as he
saw it had a visionary quality which sent him back to Dorset with—as
he wrote—'with magic in my eyes'.

In the novel that sprang immediately from his visits to St Juliot—*A
Pair of Blue Eyes*—Hardy drew on his new discoveries to add to his
scenic range. Boscastle was thinly disguised as 'Castle Boterel' and
Beeny Cliff was drawn in detail as 'the Cliff without a name'. When
Hardy returned, forty years later, it was the haunting memories of the
place that spoke directly, and now with an emotional intensity, in the
poem 'Beeny Cliff':

O the opal and the sapphire of that wandering western sea,
And the woman riding high above with bright hair flapping free—
The woman whom I loved so, and who loyally loved me.

Robert Gittings, in *The Older Hardy*, has shown how Hardy
gradually evolved a private mythology of his own, composed of
personal events and relationships and associations with particular
places. It is this which adds a further dimension to his Wessex. Among
the many dramas, great and small, that are chronicled in his stories
and his verses, and that illuminate the length and breadth of Wessex,
there moves one other drama—his own—sometimes opaque, at other
times transparent, deeply personal and moving with the suppleness of
a poet's imagination from reality to dream, and back again from dream
to reality. When his creation of Wessex was completed he was himself
so enmeshed in it as to play a dual role—as not only the observer but
the observed.

For that reason I am presenting him to you as a regional writer, but
not a provincial one. His cultural Mecca was London and a large part
of his life was spent here. His aim was clearly stated, that 'that which is
apparently local should be really universal'. In Wessex he had, in his

own words, 'enough human nature for one man's literary purpose.'
But more than that—he had an ancestral rootedness, an uncommonly
vivid sense of place and of personal involvement with it. He incar-
nated and made articulate a region which was his natural heritage.

From its countryside he drew the new aesthetic that we now speak
of as 'wilderness values'. When he considered the inevitable compari-
son of himself as a novelist with George Eliot, he claimed that she did
not touch—as he did—'the life of the fields' (to use his own phrase).
So much of the tradition in the English novel that he inherited had
been contained inside the existing social order, making that the arena
for comedy or satire or moral indignation. It was ill-fitted to accommodate the loneliness of the individual soul: it belonged, as it were,
indoors and among company. What Hardy's Wessex introduced was a
landscape where solitude and the immensities of spiritual travail could
be a normal condition—in story or in poem. 'Where one's next
neighbour is the sky', he wrote, 'mind-chains do not clank'—a
characteristically Hardyesque turn of phrase.

It was to the hills that he lifted up his eyes for salvation—or at any
rate for the serenity of a liberated spirit—to those downland hilltops
and rolling chalk contours that inspired similar feelings in Richard
Jefferies and in W. H. Hudson. And among the murmuring rustic
voices that provide the accompanying background of his Wessex,
there is the private voice of Hardy himself, making a poet's incanta-
tion of those personal symbols which form his mythology—the 'cliff
without a name' in Lyonnesse, the 'tall-spired town' which is Salisbury, the childhood scenes of Yell'ham Bottom and Froomside Vale.

If any one poem can suggest this complexity and richness of
imagination I think it must be 'Wessex Heights'. It is a poem in which
his apartness and his absorption are finely balanced. It takes us into
the secret places of the landscape where Time is immemorially past
but also instantly present.

I should like to conclude by reading it to you:

There are some heights in Wessex, shaped as if by a kindly hand
For thinking, dreaming, dying on, and at crises when I stand,
Say, on Ingpen Beacon eastward, or on Wylls-Neck westwardly,
I seem where I was before my birth, and after death may be.

In the lowlands I have no comrade, not even the lone man's friend—
Her who suffereth long and is kind; accepts what he is too weak to
    mend:

Down there they are dubious and askance; there nobody thinks as I,
But mind-chains do not clank where one's next neighbour is the sky.

In the towns I am tracked by phantoms having weird detective
    ways—
Shadows of beings who fellowed with myself of earlier days:
They hang about at places, and they say harsh heavy things—
Men with a wintry sneer, and women with tart disparagings.

Down there I seem to be false to myself, my simple self that was,
And is not now, and I see him watching, wondering what crass cause
Can have merged him into such a strange continuator as this,
Who yet has something in common with himself, my chrysalis.

I cannot go to the great grey Plain; there's a figure against the moon,
Nobody sees it but I, and it makes my breast beat out of tune;
I cannot go to the tall-spired town, being barred by the forms now
    passed
For everybody but me, in whose long vision they stand there fast.

There's a ghost at Yell'ham Bottom chiding loud at the fall of the
    night,
There's a ghost in Froom-side Vale, thin-lipped and vague, in a
    shroud of white,
There is one in the railway train whenever I do not want it near,
I see its profile against the pane, saying what I would not hear.

As for one rare fair woman, I am now but a thought of hers,
I enter her mind and another thought succeeds me that she prefers;
Yet my love for her in its fulness she herself even did not know;
Well, time cures hearts of tenderness, and now I can let her go.

So I am found on Ingpen Beacon, or on Wylls-Neck to the west,
Or else on homely Bulbarrow, or little Pilsdon Crest,
Where men have never cared to haunt, nor women have walked with
    me,
And ghosts then keep their distance; and I know some liberty.

Giff Edmonds Memorial Lecture

SHAW AND BIOGRAPHY: THE UNWRITTEN LIFE

MICHAEL HOLROYD FRHistS, FRSL

Read 16th June 1982:
Hon. C. M. Woodhouse, DSO, OBE, FRSL, in the Chair

EARLY in his *Sixteen Self-Sketches*, Bernard Shaw offers his readers an apology. It's a Shavian apology. People, he writes, kept asking him why he didn't publish his own biography. 'I reply,' he wrote, 'that I am not at all interesting biographically. I have never killed anybody. Nothing very unusual has happened to me.' To justify a biography, he went on, the subject must have had adventures. Exceptional things ought to happen to him. Dragons he should slay. 'I have had no heroic adventures,' Shaw admitted. Ninety-nine point five percent of his life, he believed, was the same as ninety-nine point five percent of everyone else's; the same familiar process of growing, feeding, excreting, dressing and undressing, lodging and moving. To inflict such a stale programme on the reader would be unforgivably tedious. Of course there was that point-five percent that was uniquely Shavian. But Shaw himself had panned these freckles of gold into his work: 'my goods are all in the bookshop window and on the stage,' he declared: 'what is communicable has been already communicated . . .'

Taking Shaw's opinions literally, you are led to the conclusion that only men of action—admirals, boy-scout leaders, wing-commanders and the like—merit a biography. As with *Boys' Own Annual*, biography is adventure-story or it is nothing. It bulges with the boastings of quacks as if they were heroes and saints, Shaw complained, in his Preface to *Back to Methuselah*, 'and of barren scoundrels as explorers and discoverers.' And of course Shaw was historically correct. In the Preface to *Androcles and the Lion*, for instance, he treats the gospels as examples of early biography. He notes how St Matthew tends ('like most biographers,' he says) to 'identify the opinions and prejudices of his hero with his own.' But Shaw also analyses St John's formula for treating biography as a record of the 'fulfilment of ancient Jewish prophesies.' In other words biography was deeply prejudiced and had its place primarily as a pointillist dot in the divinely pre-ordained picture-pattern of history. Rearrange the dots and you have altered history. And that, in a sense, was Shaw's game.

For centuries, with a few modifications reflecting changes in taste and fashion, biography had been employed to promote much the same purpose. Beginning as praise, it had developed during medieval European times into a laudatory chronicle celebrating a successful life: the life of a ruler or saint. This was part of the process of idealisation that Shaw attacked so brilliantly in *The Quintessence of Ibsenism*. If only, he implies, the tradition of biography could have found some different subjects to enshrine: the common murderer perhaps. His modest disclaimer—'I have never killed anybody'—is made in a spirit of anarchy as well as of paradox. For in Victorian times, having recovered from the shock of Boswell and Johnson, and having hounded Froude for his *Carlyle*, biography had settled back into a lavish white-washing exercise. In this assiduous effort of spring cleaning, the stains of history were continually being bleached away. That is why Shaw wanted us, the readers, suddenly to find a dead body on the carpet. After all, what else were biographers otherwise than a conglomeration of housekeepers adroit in the art of tidying away all specks of human nature? The house they kept so smartly spic-and-span was a museum dedicated to the past, not a living place: it was a Madame Tussauds filled with the waxwork figures of regularly-dusted monarchs and statesmen, their medals and crowns for ever wonderfully polished and glittering. Shaw wanted to complement this palace of standard celebrities with a chamber of horrors—not in the interests of improving the art of biography but in order to make biography a useful tool in changing the picture of history: rearranging the dots. Like St John he has a formula; like St Matthew his heroes—Ibsen, Wagner, Julius Caesar—are made to illustrate his opinions.

As a man-of-letters who craved to influence the political climate of Britain, Ireland and the world, Shaw believed in the power of words to enforce action: that, perhaps, was his romanticism. He proposed that biographers should exchange one package of myths for another—an up-to-date package that would set human beings in a new context. No longer should biography be controlled by prophesies from the past; it must be connected to our future aspirations. It is part of a humane process of helping us to realise our hopes. If the word is preferable to the deed it is because, as Shaw wrote, 'only on paper has humanity yet achieved glory, beauty, truth, knowledge, virtue, and abiding love.' But then, as Oscar Wilde had suggested, life imitates art, reality pursues the dream. That, in Shaw's mind, was the justification for a life spent writing down words on paper.

Shaw had pleaded guilty to having 'never killed anybody,' but many Victorian heroes of biographies had of course, directly or indirectly, killed a good number of people. The body Shaw demands to be placed on the carpet, though a shockingly untidy sight for a fastidious person such as himself, sheds no blood. However untraditionally introduced, it is still a waxwork. For Shaw was that strange creature: the passive revolutionary. His thought is bold; his feelings are timid. Intellectually he travelled everywhere; emotionally he stayed at home. His audacious paper paradoxes are built from this inconsistency of thought and feeling. You may spot his emotional immaturity in much of his work. *Arms and the Man*, for example, is precociously clever; but it is a war of chocolate soldiers as seen from the nursery. His vocabulary is another symptom. He writes of biography as being devoted to 'scoundrels'—and with that word we are immediately back again in *Boys' Own Annual*. It is a world he never wholly left and it accounts for his view of biography as being best suited to adventurers. While he responds emotionally to these boastful tales of warriors and quacks, intellectually he condemns such exercises. Often, he tells us, biography displays the very worst aspect of immaturity: a gratuitous and uncomprehending cruelty. 'Can anything be more disgusting,' he asks in his Preface to *Misalliance*, 'than the spectacle of a nation reading the biography of Gladstone and gloating over the account of how he was flogged at Eton, two of his schoolfellows being compelled to hold him down whilst he was flogged.' Shaw's argument is that the vicarious pleasure of such sadistic descriptions helped to endorse an indecent routine which we honoured with the name education. This education had produced 'an

England of ignoramuses' he wrote, '. . . [content] to be driven day after day into compounds and set to the tasks they loathe by the men they hate and fear, as if this were the inevitable destiny of mankind. And naturally, when they grow up, they helplessly exchange the prison of the school for the prison of the mine or the workshop or the office, and drudge along stupidly and miserably, with just enough gregarious instinct to turn furiously on any intelligent person who proposes a change.' Old fashioned immature biography taught its readers a different story. Gladstone was flogged; Gladstone became Prime Minister. Perhaps if your son was flogged sufficiently, held down by his schoolfellows as Gladstone had been, he too might become Prime Minister, or Foreign Secretary, or at least Chancellor of the Duchy of Lancaster. By these naive and primitive methods, biography idealised a corrupt system; by enhaloing such barbarities with myths biography helped to perpetuate the corruption. You may see from this the potential power Shaw believed lay in biography. He was with Carlyle in thinking that our very history was 'the essence of innumerable biographies.' In the past biography had largely existed as an instrument for maintaining the *status quo*. In the future it could be a vehicle for progress. Shaw seemed to have high hopes of progress. 'It would be quite easy to make England a paradise, according to our present ideas, in a few years,' he wrote shortly before the First World War. 'There is no mystery about it . . . The difficulty is not the way but the will. And we have no will because the first thing done with us in childhood was to break our will.'

Shaw's will had not been broken: but his emotions had been lamed. He felt he was unlovable: he felt that, since this was the unalterable factor in his life, the only thing he could do was to make a virtue of his unlovableness, put it to some use for people. He would sit endlessly on committees, make of himself an ascetic and an hygienic example in matters of diet and clothing, puncture the amiable pretence of romanticism with his plays, turn the world uncomfortably upside down for the good of its inhabitants. In short, he would encourage people to become self-sufficient rather than depend for their vital happiness on the off-chance of love. He would make a world fit for the unlovable. He would give them (via the State) money; he would give them self-respect; he would give them everything but love. And it was true that he was unlovable; but then, looking around, so were most people. Only by means of paradox, for a moment or two, here and there, in their jokes perhaps, might they appear to earn love. But it was reality, not appearances, Shaw believed himself to be concerned with—though one might have to exploit appearances in order to change the realities of the world. 'I implore you not to describe me as "a lovable human being",' he begged one of his American biographers Lawrence Langner who went on to publish a book called *G.B.S. and the Lunatic*. To justify acting like this on his instinct of self-dislike, he gave a characteristically commonsense reason. To do otherwise, he said, to appear generous, for example, would bring him a million begging letters by the next post. So, he instructed Langner to present him as detestable, avaricious, merciless, contemptuous and every-thing odious enough to discourage people from writing to him. 'Otherwise you may hasten my already imminent death.' As a child he had been neglected; as an adult he possessed an uncontrollable craving for attention; and long before the end this craving disgusted him. It was not a vanity. It was not people's good opinion he wanted: simply their attention. 'Woe unto me when all men praise me!' he makes St Joan say. Against the universal praise of others Shaw had an impreg-nable defence: he exorbitantly praised himself. There was no room for others. 'Why should I get another man to praise me,' he asks in the Preface to *Three Plays for Puritans*, 'when I can praise myself.' But his praise did not mirror any high self-esteem: it was, like so much else in Shaw, a compensation for something else. His very optimism was founded on paradox.

The Shavian paradox reflects the rift between his intellectual and emotional self; and his attitude to biography underlines this incon-sistency. He had been adamant, for example, about how uninteresting he was biographically—and then stuck this statement by way of Shavian advertisement at the beginning of a volume of autobiog-raphical sketches. Of course it is true that he never wrote, as it were, an official autobiography. He was quite ineligible, he said. Yet his miscellaneous writings about himself were so appallingly copious that when, after his death, a selection of them was prepared for publication by Stanley Weintraub, it ran two sturdy volumes: some six hundred pages in all. For in fact it was not true that ninety-nine point five percent of Shaw's existence was the same as ninety-nine point five percent of everyone else's. Its very foundations were different. His childhood was unusual; his marriage was unusual; what he wore, what he ate, even what he failed to drink—all were unusual. He was an isolated man, out of touch with Ireland, with England, and the world he wished to influence. In a curiously moving passage in the Preface to his novel *Immaturity*, he writes: 'if I am to be entirely communicative on this subject I must add that the mere rawness which soon rubs off was complicated by a deeper strangeness which has made me all my life a sojourner on this planet rather than a native of it. Whether it be that I was born mad or a little too sane, my kingdom was not of this world: I was at home only in the realm of my imagination, and at my ease only with the mighty dead.' And yet he told his biographer Archibald Henderson that 'unless you can show me in the context of my time as a member of a very interesting crowd you will fail to produce the only thing that makes biography tolerable.' What he wanted from his biographers was a vehicle for his thought that would place it in the current of contemporary life and make him a representative being, 'a member of a very interesting crowd,' no longer a strange sojourner on this planet but a native at ease with the living rather than the dead. He wanted his life recreated on the page with the facts brought up to date.

Shaw distrusted biographers: and his distrust is not difficult to explain. He believed that the source of all our ideas lay in our instinct; that we used our minds to explain the promotings of this instinct and to convince other people of the validity of our ideas. Ideas that were not put into practice lay for ever in the womb. It was a test of our will to get these ideas received into the laws of the country. In the dialectics of debating pretty well no one, not even G. K. Chesterton, certainly not H. G. Wells, could get the better of Shaw. He was brilliant. And he worked enormously hard. No one who has looked at his work for the Fabian Society or as a St Pancras Vestryman, can doubt the strength and stamina of his will. Yet although he stimulated several generations of young people to question the ideas of their parents and to begin thinking for themselves, almost none of his political ideas, from the new alphabet to equality of income (pay, that is, without differentials) and the Coupled Vote (voting, that is, for a man-and-woman) came near to being implemented. Shaw wanted his ideas tested in practice; he did not want them merely traced biographically back to their source. There was only one evil in the world, he argued, against which we were powerless: and that was the tampering with our instincts when we were children. If the compass of these instincts was no longer true then we were, to use the title of one of his plays, *On the Rocks*. The fundamental question of Shaw's life was whether the course he was attempting to steer us on was true or false.

To show that his ideas had grown naturally from the social and political soil of mid-nineteenth century Britain, Shaw gives us a picture of his parents that is typical, he says, of the marriages made under the economic conditions of those times. His mother and father married for love—for love of money. This sounds eccentric, but then how few people, Shaw reasons, living in the strict religious and class stratification of Victorian Ireland were free to do anything else. So his parents married conventionally and then after twenty-one years—a very reasonable time—they parted amicably because they could not afford, after launching a family of three, to continue living together. They had, like so many others, miscalculated financially. They were never divorced. People didn't go in for divorces in those days. Besides there was no need: no particular quarrel, no lovers' parting. Such things were mainly confined to the pages of romantic novels. Shaw's father drank a bit—so do many fathers. But on the whole his parents got on well enough. You could say of them—as you could say of him—that ninety-nine point five percent of their lives were like ninety-nine point five percent of everyone else's lives at that time. It was the times that were wrong, and it was the times that Shaw set out to change. He described his childhood as 'rich only in dreams, frightful & loveless in realities.' At the age of twenty he turned his back on dreams, on the gathering celtic twilight of Ireland, and set out in England, through the body of his literary and political work, to make the realities less frightful. That, in rough-and-ready terms, is Shaw's account of how his work developed from the experiences of his early years.

   Yet it is possible for a biographer to tell a different story that shows G.B.S. substituting financial need for emotional impulse and charts his thought as a fantastical development of his early dreams. In this story, Shaw secretly believes himself to have inherited from his parents qualities that were so incompatible as to drive them, even after twenty-one years of marriage, to inhabit different countries. His gift for drama came from making external these inherited differences; and his mission, like a religious quest, was to find a synthesis between these conflicting forces. The Superman became his symbol of this synthesis; and the great debates of his plays—between the Devil and Don Juan in *Man and Superman*; between Undershaft and Barbara in *Major Barbara*; between Father Keegan and Larry Doyle in *John Bull's Other Island*—were attempts to reconcile such incompatibilities. He searched for a way of uniting word and deed, spirit and body, heart and mind, the actual with the ideal, reality with the dream. In

John Bull's Other Island he makes Larry Doyle, the Irishman who had come to England, say: 'Live in contact with dreams and you will get something of their charm: live in contact with facts and you will get something of their brutality. I wish I could find a country to live in where the facts were not brutal and the dreams not unreal.' There is such a place, of course, and its name is Utopia. And Utopia would be England when England became a paradise. It was, Shaw had predicted 'quite easy to make England a paradise.' But he had said that before the First World War. After that war, during which he wrote *Heartbreak House*, he no longer believed this. Our collective instinct had been trivialised, he felt, and was leading us astray. Increasingly his ideas depended on a sacrifice of the actual present for the hypothetical future. If there were brutalities—brutalities, let us say, in Soviet Russia—who were we to point to them in virtuous indignation, we who had so recently gloated over Gladstone's flogging at Eton? When had history been anything but brutal? When had human beings ever treated themselves with consideration? Truly we were an unlovable species. It might be better if, like the pterodactyl and tyrannosaurus, we were quietly phased out of the evolutionary process. After the Zeppelin raid at the end of *Heartbreak House* the survivors are almost disappointed to be still alive. 'What a glorious experience!' gasps Mrs Hushabye. 'I hope they'll come again tomorrow night.' And Ellie Dunn breathes, radiant at the prospect, 'Oh, I hope so.' And that's the end of the play.

Human Beings were unwilling, perhaps incapable of learning much—though, of course, Shaw added, we must keep on trying. 'I am by nature and destiny a preacher,' says Aubrey at the end of *Too True to be Good*. '. . . But I have no Bible, no creed: the war has shot both out of my hands . . . meanwhile my gift has possession of me: I must preach and preach and preach no matter how late the hour and how short the day, no matter whether I have nothing to say—.' Though he retained a patina of optimism, Shaw's creed had gone in *Back to Methuselah* where he finally divorces spirit from body, like Ariel released from Prospero, the genius from the gentleman. The Superman had now become a Prometheus, bound to a rock of inactivity by the fetters of bureaucracy: a frustrated believer in action whose Demogorgon is to be some modern dictator—Stalin, or Mussolini or even Hitler. It is the predicament that the Devil has warned us against in *Man and Superman*: 'Beware of the pursuit of the Superhuman: it leads to an indiscriminate contempt for the human.' In the guise of Don Juan, Shaw's sin was to have treated men and women as if they were outside the moral world, like pet cats and dogs. His kindness, which was persistent, derived from no love of his neighbour but from the striving, by way of example, for moral superiority conferred by impeccable good manners. So ends the story.

It is the sort of story Shaw feared, suggesting as it does that the divorce of body and spirit in *Back to Methuselah* was almost pre-ordained by the splitting up of his parents; that his early years were so irregular as to have produced in him a wayward philosophy. One can detect this fear in his treatment of the two biographers whose books he stopped from publication. The first was by a fantastical character called Demetrius O'Bolger, the son of an Irish Police Inspector, who began his study in 1912 as a thesis for the Graduate Department of the University of Pennsylvania where, apparently, he had been a student for fifteen years. He was an admirer of Shaw and had previously approached him for advice on how to become a playwright. He had convinced Shaw, by his proposal to add an extra Act to *Fanny's First Play*, that he was fundamentally a madman. Apparently encouraged by this, Shaw agreed to answer his questions and O'Bolger, vastly pleased, decided to scrutinise Shaw's youth in Dublin. 'In a general way I adopted the policy of following up loose threads in the studies of Mr Shaw that had been made by others,' he explained. 'I determined to run out the thread of his home surroundings . . . I thought I saw not a few reticences . . . and I determined to penetrate them and systema-tize the results if Mr Shaw were willing to give me the necessary information.'

And Shaw, like Barkis, was willing. What was there to fear from a madman? O'Bolger would send him a sheet of paper with a question typed at the top, and Shaw would fill the rest of the page with an answer sometimes running to five or six hundred words. His help grew almost into an obstacle preventing O'Bolger from completing anything. In fact, the poor man often completed his book—though never to anyone's satisfaction. He completed it, for example, in February 1916, only to receive, a little later that month, a twenty-nine page typewritten letter from Shaw describing the circumstances of his youth and the household in which he grew up. The death of his mother, Shaw explained, had to some extent untied his hands. Certainly he had never been so forthcoming. But he did not send these pages for publication as they stood, he added. He was simply giving

O'Bolger access to a few hasty autobiographical sketches that he might possibly elaborate and publish himself later on.

After another two years or so O'Bolger again completed his work. A few months after the armistice of 1918 he received an offer from Harper Brothers to publish a revised text. He sent the news to Shaw and sat down to make a fourth draft, working 'till the nerves of neck and the back of my head could no longer stand the strain.' Harpers seemed delighted; but Shaw was not. He had not written all that matter to enable Harper Brothers to make a huge profit at O'Bolger's expense and his own. He demanded to see the contract and, having been sent it, confirmed that if the book contained a line of which the copyright belonged to him he would treat it as an infringement. As a result, Harpers cancelled the contract. This was exactly what Shaw wanted them to do. But it was not what O'Bolger wanted. Shaw, he noted, 'had delivered a sound blow for principle's sake. He had saved me from being fleeced by saving me from being published.' In a frantic letter, O'Bolger alternately abused Shaw and begged him to change his mind. Shaw responded by cautioning him not to be scared. After all, he was merely suffering from a sort of delirium tremens brought on by overwork. This advice sounded to O'Bolger like that of a doctor who prescribes for a bankrupt invalid six luxurious weeks on the French Riviera. He retorted angrily that not all American publishers were eager to bring out books about G.B.S., apparently unaware how pleased Shaw would be to hear this. Another American publisher, however, did express interest in the manuscript and asked for a Shavian Preface—but Shaw refused to authorise the book in this way. It was no longer ostensibly a question of contracts, but of the text. He had been provoked by O'Bolger into revealing more about his early years than ever before. Perhaps he had felt a *need* to write some of it down following his mother's death. But he did not want to see it all in print especially when so many details were interfered with by O'Bolger. So he held on to the manuscript. It was still in his possession in 1922. Somehow he could not make up his mind to send 'that blasted MS of yours' back without another look at it. Looking at it again, Shaw decided that O'Bolger had pressed into the service of literature all his father's police techniques. This explained his treatment of Shaw's parents as suspicious characters in custody, his rejection of all Shaw's statements as unsupported by evidence and coming from a tainted source and so on.

According to Shaw his biographer was suffering from something

very common in Ireland, a Resentment Complex. He had the resentment of the poor man against the rich man, of the Irish Catholic
against the Irish Protestant, and several other resentments from which
he had achieved a portrait of a most horrible woman whom he alleged
was Shaw's mother, with a sordid husband, and a disingenuous son,
forming the sort of Irish interior which he most hated and despised as
typifying every social injustice from which he and his people ever
suffered.

What emerges from this response is Shaw's genuine distress.
O'Bolger's impressions had been composed from Shaw's letters: he
had turned the paradoxes inside out to produce an ugly picture of the
formative Dublin years—those years that Shaw himself had admitted
were 'frightful in realities.' So they reached deadlock. Shaw allowed
that O'Bolger was entitled to his opinions, but not to Shaw's endorse-
ment of them to the extent of gaining immunity from the copyright
and libel laws. Under those conditions no publisher would agree to
print the book and so, at last, O'Bolger submitted to the process of
Shavian editing and amendment that all other biographers were
obliged to accept. Unfortunately this involved practically rewriting
his book for him, Shaw later explained, and for that it was impossible
for him to find time. So the manuscript, now in its fifth draft, and
called *The Real Shaw*, remained suspended: a great vexation to both
of them. 'You will certainly be the death of me,' Shaw cried out with
what was to be the most lethal of his paradoxes. In the summer of
1923, O'Bolger suddenly died. Shaw did not know whether to be glad
or sorry. The situation had been a painful one for him and a great
worry for O'Bolger whom it had helped to worry into his grave. A
tragic business, Shaw concluded; but his biographer had been unhelp-
able.

O'Bolger had made no startling discoveries about these years in
Ireland, but his enquiries had pressed on a bruise, startled Shaw,
made him deftly rearrange the facts as if to wrap up some wound. And
having rearranged the facts he stuck to them. The source of his
difficulties lay in the unorthodox menage-à-trois in which he was
brought up. His mother shared the house with two Georges: the
alcoholic redundant Civil Servant George Carr Shaw; and the musical
phenomenon George John Vandeleur Lee. After which George was
G.B.S. named? The question seems to have arisen in Shaw's mind
uncomfortably enough for him to have laid special emphasis on his
resemblance to his father, to have eliminated George as his own name

('Don't George me') and to have crowded his plays with characters whose parentage is dubious. But if, as seems almost certain, Shaw was the son of George Carr Shaw, then G.B.S., the public figure, was modelled on the phenomenal Vandeleur Lee. His mother's happiness, not just her economic survival, had centred on Lee. Shaw feared too much biographical detective work into these years because it might revive old suspicions and reveal new facts.

He did no research himself, he confessed to St John Ervine who wanted in the mid 1930s to write a Life of Shaw, for he had found that, if he invented all his facts on the basis of his knowledge of human nature, he always came out right, whereas, if he referred to documents and authorities, they wearied him and set him wrong. Writers should trust their genius rather than their industry, he thought. It was the less fallible of the two. St John Ervine's reputation for industrious research seems to have set Shaw against his book. Ervine stopped work on it in 1942 when Shaw dismissed what he had written about his Irish years as 'hopeless'. He seemed interested not in individuals but only in their classes, Shaw told him. Yet, elsewhere he had insisted on being placed in what he called 'the context of my time,' had suggested that his parents' marriage was characteristic of their class and emphasised the ordinariness of his upbringing. Expounding on the matter of class, he informed Ervine that Vandeleur Lee 'had no creed. I never heard him mention religion.' If this is literally true, it is nevertheless socially and factually misleading. For the documents and authorities Shaw advised Ervine to ignore, reveal Lee to have been a Roman Catholic. This was no matter of religious principle, but a fact of social life in Dublin. The menage-à-trois was therefore composed of two Protestants and a Catholic—as noticeable in Ireland in the mid-nineteenth century as a household of mixed-colour in England in the early twentieth century. This was the sort of fact from which Shaw wanted St John Ervine's attention diverted—since Ervine, being Irish himself, would understand the implications very well.

This is a good example of what Shaw wanted to forget and a good illustration of how he wanted his biographers to create a better past for him. But now that he can no longer suffer from the consequences, it is possible to put some of the facts back in their original places. The first person to have begun this job was a strange character called B. C. Rosset. He was an American somewhat in the tradition of Demetrius O'Bolger. He was no writer; his book, published briefly in 1964, also in Pennsylvania, and called *Shaw of Dublin: The Formative Years*, is a compendium of research on precisely the lines envisaged by O'Bolger. But since there was no Shaw to assist him to distraction, Rosset did something that neither O'Bolger nor even St John Ervine had done. He went to Dublin. He did more. He rented a room in the Synge Street house where Shaw was born; he married the cook in Trinity College Dublin and he settled down to work in every cobwebbed archive of the city. And he made the discoveries that O'Bolger was looking for over forty years earlier. For example, Shaw had written that Vandeleur Lee 'had to make his position in London before he could provide the musical setting for my mother and sister.' It was Rosset who found from the list of departures for Holyhead printed in *The Irish Times* that Mrs Shaw followed Lee to London on her twenty-first wedding anniversary—that is only a few days after Lee's own departure, not the months or even year or two that Shaw implied. But the hand of Shaw appeared to stretch back and shut this book of Rosset's almost as decisively as it had O'Bolger's. Rosset had quoted from Shaw without the permission of the Shaw Estate, and the Shaw Estate swiftly withdrew the book from publication. Not long after that Rosset died. The history of Demetrius O'Bolger seemed to have been posthumously repeated.

Besides marrying his cook, Rosset had made one other inspired choice while living in Dublin. He had selected a man called John O'Donovan as his research assistant. Many of his finds were in fact the discoveries of John O'Donovan who, unlike Rosset, was a natural writer. He wrote a play about Shaw's youth for the Abbey Theatre and a tiny luminous masterpiece of biographical detective work, a study of Vandeleur Lee and his influence on G.B.S. entitled *Shaw and the Charlatan Genius*.

How would Shaw himself have responded to such a book? His attitude to biography had altered in the course of his life. As a young anonymous reviewer for the *Pall Mall Gazette* in the 1880s, he had called for the sort of revolution in biographical writing that Lytton Strachey was to conduct. Later, in 1905, he wrote, to Henry Irving's son: 'If you write a life of your father, don't make it a vestryman's epitaph. Let us have the truth about the artist—the stupendously selfish, self-sacrificing truth. The artist sacrifices everything to his art, beginning with himself. But the art *is* himself.' In this statement Shaw's attitude is on the turn. For what he is really beginning to say is that biography should support the work, if necessary at the expense of the life; that it should (as with the gospel of St John) fulfil the career of the artist which takes over from the life of the man. Later still, he refers to 'the dramatic faculty that enables me to see the stage effect I am producing, & to exploit it histrionically for the inner purpose that drives me on without any real complicity in its artificiality.' And yet, since you may not separate style from content in art, there is a complicity. Artificial histrionics had become part of his reality. In his next sentence he writes: 'Reality has no place in individual portraits because Reality is not an individual thing: it drives me on as it drives everyone else.' But then he crossed out 'Reality' and substituted 'the inner life.' Shaw knew that reality and the inner life were the same thing; but he over-rode them with stage effect and the external life. He knew the sort of distortion this was likely to produce. In his fifties he had written that 'no man has an accurate knowledge of his own life, & that when an autobiography does not agree with a biography, the biography is probably right and the autobiography wrong.' Such a statement, from someone who invariably imposed autobiography on his biographers, is devastating. The self-sacrificing truth of the artist turns out to be the sacrifice of truth to the art of Dr Pangloss. The man, who in the nineteenth century, had called for a new type of truth-telling in biography had grown into a twentieth century subject for biographies wryly reminding his readers that 'when you read a biography remember that the truth is never fit for publication.'

In so far as this was valid in Shaw's lifetime, it cannot have the same validity now that he is dead and unable personally to suffer from what is written about him. One thing, however, has not changed in the seventy-five years since Archibald Henderson began the first authorised biography of Shaw. On a visit to England, Henderson was introduced to Bram Stoker as Bernard Shaw's biographer. 'I can only say,' remarked Stoker, 'that you have my profoundest sympathy!' That need of sympathy for Shaw's biographer is, I can assure you from my heart, as profound today as it was then.

Giff Edmonds Memorial Lecture

BEATRICE WEBB: THE NOVELIST WHO NEVER WAS

NORMAN MACKENZIE FRSL

Read 15th June 1983:
Sir Angus Wilson, CBE, CLit, FRSL, in the Chair

WHEN the first volume of Beatrice Webb's *Diary* was published (October 1982) several reviewers came to much the same conclusion about her and her skills as a writer. A glamorous George Eliot, Jane Marcus called her in the *New York Times*, 'a diarist with the obvious gifts of a novelist.' The diaries, José Harris said in the *TLS*, 'combine the moral insight of a George Eliot with the malice of an Evelyn Waugh'—an intriguing combination that set me speculating about such hybrid titles as *Passfield Revisited* and *Pink Mischief*! Some papers saw her more as a fictional character than as author. The *Melbourne Age* thought the handsome and intelligent Beatrice was more 'a classic Henry James heroine . . . the Isobel Archer of the English political life', while the *Washington Post* described her as 'a socialistic Jane Eyre'. But Claire Tomalin told us in the *Sunday Times* that, had she married Joseph Chamberlain, 'the world might possibly have gained a novelist and lost a Fabian policymaker' and the *Economist* agreed that 'long entries in the diary show what a novelist she might have been'.

This is a notion that Samuel Hynes put strongly in an essay published ten years ago in *Edwardian Occasions*. 'Beatrice Webb', he said, 'was an artist who never wrote a work of art . . . she might have

been a considerable novelist, a sort of latter-day George Eliot.' The
more I read the diary the more this thought recurs, and I find myself
wondering about the quirks of personality and circumstance that
tipped such a remarkable talent away from the privacies of literature
and into public life. If Beatrice had been able to let her fancy run away
with her, instead of harnessing it to Fabian purposes, she would have
begun her career as a writer as a contemporary of Mrs Humphry Ward
and finished it at the same time as Virginia Woolf: one can only begin
to guess at the unnumbered books she might have written over the
years between. For besides all the learned history and energetic
reform that characterised the immensely productive Webb partnership, Beatrice found time to write well over two million words in
her barely legible manuscript diary. Perhaps we should not regret her
loss in an age so prodigal of literary gifts—perhaps those of us who
have benefited from her other creations, especially the London
School of Economics and the *New Statesman*, should be content that
her energies took a more practical turn. And yet there is so much in
this diary that makes me think of that might-have-been that I make no
apology for spending an hour reflecting upon it.

The diary itself, of course, covers an extraordinary span of time and
a great range of ideas and experience. Beatrice began it in 1873, when
she was the eighth and fifteen year-old daughter of an enlightened
railway promoter; and she made the last entry less than a fortnight
before her death in April 1943, after half a century of marriage to
Sidney Webb and of joint dedication to progressive social science. But
it is far more than a chronicle that interweaves the private and public
events of a lifetime that stretched from *The Origin of Species* to the
discovery of nuclear energy—surprisingly more, indeed, for those
who had previously dismissed Beatrice as Mrs Grundy in pink
petticoats and were astonished by what they discovered in the diary.

It begins like any adolescent girl's diary, with shy confessions and
confidences, though even the early entries reveal a remarkable command of language for a child thought to be dull and unsuitable for
schooling. It passes through the doldrums of self-education, where it
might well have foundered under the weight of passages copied from
Stubbs, comments on Goethe and notes on the galleries of Florence.
They are the kind of entries that Miss Honeychurch might have
written in her earnest unawakened years. And then the diary is
overwhelmed by a storm of passion, as an unacceptable and unfulfilled
attachment to Joseph Chamberlain drives Beatrice relentlessly to

explore and then control her feelings. After an unhappy childhood, she wrote in 1901, came 'the catastrophe of my life'.

The long agony of that infatuation cries out of these scribbled pages, and echoes again and again through all that follow them. For it transforms the diary. Once Beatrice comes to understand and accept what she called her 'duplex personality' she begins to use the diary as the hidden or 'Other' self, and the ensuing tension is the spring that might have driven her as a novelist if she had not found a governor in her marriage to Sidney Webb.

She was well aware of this conflict. She spoke of the struggle between 'the Ego that affirms and the Ego that denies' in the opening sentence of *My Apprenticeship*, which was the only work of literary significance that she completed and saw published. Marriage, which she more than once described as a form of suicide, certainly had a killing effect upon her imagination, even if it provided a means to sublimate her emotional energies into a creed and craft of social reform. 'When Sidney is with me I cannot talk to the "Other Self" with whom I commune when I am alone', she wrote in October 1904: ' "It" ceases to be present and only reappears when he is absent. Then the "Old Self", who knew me and whom I have known for that long period before Sidney entered my life, who seems to be that which is permanent in me, sits again in the judgement seat and listens to the tale of the hours and the days, acts, thoughts and feelings which the Earthly One has experienced.'

It was only in the diary—only in the diary and not even in intimate conversation—that Beatrice was willing to cast the balance of her paradoxical nature, so that these irregular entries become a running ledger of her crowded life. As one succeeds another we see her sexual desires at war with her moral convictions, her instinctive mysticism struggling with her educated idea of a positive science of society, her strong and essentially individualist conscience wrestling with her belief in the collective regulation of behaviour, her almost frenetic energy alternating with bouts of anorexic and depressive ill-health. A woman who so divided her life, in order to cope with its temptations and its troubles, found nothing incongruous in making her diary her psychic partner to complement the prosaic but purposeful working partnership with Sidney.

Yet from time to time Beatrice glimpsed an alternative. In 1883, she began to feel her powers as a writer. In November of that year, she visited Bacup, the little mill town where her mother's family had risen from clogs to riches; and in the long letters she then wrote to her father it is clear that her latent literary talents are emerging. She begins to set scenes and give them a dramatic emphasis, to sketch characters in a few sentences, to structure and to sustain a narrative, to make a point without labouring it.

I think it is significant that this visit came soon after Beatrice met Chamberlain. Her perceptions seem to have been sharpened by falling in love, and for the next stressful years the diary entries show her experimenting with ways of expressing what she saw and felt. They are increasingly concerned with her work in the East End, and then with the tedious domestic routines forced on her when her father was crippled by illness: she is consciously subordinating her hidden self to her growing sense of social and family duty. And yet the possibility of authorship remains.

'This last month or so', Beatrice wrote on 30th September 1889, 'I have been haunted by a longing to create characters and to move them to and fro among fictitious circumstances. To put the matter plainly —by the vulgar wish to write a novel'. It was a revealing phrase. It was much more *vulgar* to write fiction than to grind away at minute books and conference reports. When Beatrice looked back over all the novels she had read, from works of genius to the output of the penny-a-liner, she asked what all of them had accomplished for 'the advancement of society' and gave a dusty answer. Whatever the claims of Art, was not Science morally preferable and socially more desirable? Was it not better, in effect, to write *The Co-Operative Movement* than—well, she might have made an exception of *Middlemarch* or *Robert Elsmere* —than, say, *Diana of the Crossways*? It was surely better to be possessed by a 'supreme ambition' to discover and apply 'the truths about social organisation' than to satisfy the craving for what Beatrice disparagingly called 'a day's fame'.

And yet . . . for all her conviction that literary work would mean 'vanity and vexation of spirit: would begin in self-indulgence and end in a craving for popularity', Beatrice hankered after it. 'There is an immense attractiveness in the comparative ease of descriptive writing' she admitted in that same diary entry. 'Compare it with work in which movements of commodities, percentages, depreciations, averages, and all the ugly horrors of commercial facts are in the dominant place . . .' Compare. That is exactly what she did. More than once, in the privacy of the diary, when she was exhausted by a stint of research, Beatrice railed against the 'fearful drudgery' of writing the pamphlets, reports and monumental histories of local government for which the Webbs were famous.

The creative spark glowed faint, but still it glowed. 'I long sometimes for a wider culture, knowledge of other and higher forms of intellectual effort', she wrote in July 1893. 'All the world of art and literature is closed to me. But I do not see how with such slight and intermittent intellectual energy I could well spare any portion of it from my own work.' Six years later, on 1st February 1895, when she had been married for three years and she and Sidney were completing their first joint work, *The History of Trade Unionism*, Beatrice found herself longing for a change of pace and occupation. 'For the last three months', she noted, 'an idea has haunted me that after we have finished our stiff work on trade unions I would try my hand at pure "Fiction" in the form of a novel dated "60 Years Hence" . . . Two main ideas should run through it. The fully-fledged woman engaged in a great career should be pictured just as we now picture a man, and collectivism should be the orthodox creed carried out as a matter of course in moulding the institutions of the country. The truth is, I want to have my "fling"! I want to imagine anything I damn please without regard to facts as they are—I want to give full play to whatever faculty I have for descriptive and dramatic work . . . I am sick to death of trying to put hideous facts, multitudinous details, exasperating qualifications, into readable form.'

When Sidney was courting Beatrice he had once written 'I hope it will be a case of Beauty and the Beast, not Titania and Bottom', and there are moments when one feels that Beauty is chafing at the worthy but pedestrian conditions that Beast, however kindly, is imposing on her! Even the novel she had in mind was affected by the belief that all endeavours should be useful. She had first conceived it in the autumn of 1889, when she was staying with her eccentric friend, the aristocratic simple lifer, Auberon Herbert. 'Between us we started a novel, *Looking Forward*—an answer to *Looking Backward*—for which I supplied the plot and the characters, while he is to work out a reformed world on individualist lines.' In 1895, she seems to have revived that notion, even though the 'reformed world' would now reflect her conversion to a socialism much like that which Edward Bellamy had envisaged in his utopian novel.

Perhaps the Webb-reformed world of 1895 was well lost to fiction. Perhaps Beatrice's didactic impulses would have made a genuine creative release impossible. She became, after all, a noted wirepuller in London's salon politics, and a person with the instincts of a puppet-master finds it hard to set the puppets free. By then 'the longing to create characters and to move them to and fro among fictitious circumstances' had hardened into a coarser form of manipulation, and Beatrice's great talents as a writer had been trained to serve the alternative self of the diarist rather than to create the alternative worlds of the novelist.

They were, nevertheless great talents, as I hope to persuade you. She had vivid powers of observation, a good ear and an excellent memory. She had a sense of style, and a sharp turn of phrase. 'So much taste', she wrote on seeing Chamberlain's home in Birmingham for the first time. 'And all of it bad!' She could let her fancy roam before she learned to curb and condemn the kind of daydreaming she called 'castles in the air'. She had a gift of ruthless and detached appraisal which she used as unsparingly upon herself as on the relatives, friends and public acquaintances who fill her pages—an ambitious Liberal politician, an adulterous novelist, an aristocratic wife, an objectionably ardent young revolutionary, an unwordly bishop, a dishonest maid . . . there are close to three thousand characters from her *comédie humaine* sketched in the diary. She had no formal knowledge of psychology to help her. In all this torrent of words Freud and Jung are mentioned once, in a subordinate clause. But it is her gifts for characterisation—and for the epitomes that set character against circumstance—that make her writing come alive.

Nor would Beatrice have lacked for plots. The diary is a quarry from which she would have cut plots of any size—from the rambling and ramifying story of the Potter clan, whose business interests and domestic dramas overshadow those of the Forsytes, to tales which would have fitted all the genres of her day.

Imagine, for instance, how Beatrice might have begun the Potter saga with a paragraph such as this, taken from the diary for 9th October 1893:

> It is some years since I have watched summer turn into autumn and felt the first breath of winter creeping over the country. This year the summer left us early, the sky closing over with cold grey clouds, only now and again they break and the sun stands out and lights up the sombre blues and browns of the landscape . . . As I stand and watch the clouds drifting across the moor . . . memories of old days

jostle each other and seem to take me back to the thoughts and feelings of daily life of struggling girlhood . . .

And from the same year I take a possible chapter opening which describes the Potter sisterhood after the first of them had died, and does so with such powerful yet controlled hints that any novelist would be happy to fill out.

> Georgie looked the saddest of the sisters—to her, life had little charm, though on the surface so prosperous; her marriage a big mistake. Poor little Rosalind with her miserable husband, an egotistical invalid, looking depressed but sweet and loving. Mary, Margaret, Kate, all happy women. Blanche too madly noble and too nobly mad to be disturbed by death. All and each of us going our own way, saddened and softened by the common loss, perhaps even drawn together by the fear that others might drop down too. But family relationships are like to a strange dream—real and yet unreal, always disappointing and disquieting whether in shortcomings or an excess of affection without intimacy.

There are sub-plots a-plenty here. Her sister Blanche, for instance, might have been the subject of a late Victorian novel—*The Betrayed Wife*, let us say, which would have told the story of how she altruistically hanged herself so that her husband might be happy with an Italian singer. Her youngest sister Rosy's wanderings and eccentricities could make a more startling tale than those of Grant Allen's sensational *Woman Who Did*, just as Beatrice's own frustrated attachment to Chamberlain and her choice of Sidney and a career could have merged romantic and feminist fiction into a novel combination. There is, indeed, a splendid epitome of a 'Woman Question' novel in the account Beatrice gives of Carrie Darling, a governess in a sister's family.

> She was the first 'professional' woman I had come across. Fresh from Newnham and full of the fervour and enthusiasm of those early pioneers, saved from priggishness and pedantry by having earned her livelihood from fifteen years of age, by being at least three times engaged to be married before she went to college at the age of twenty-eight—with, in fact, all the charms of a bohemian and a highly-trained professional, she captivated my imagination. Her friendship was of the utmost value to me: she stimulated all that was good in me—my love of learning and intellectual ambition, all my

moral enthusiasm, and to some extent checked the vulgar material-
ism brought about by life in second-rate fashionable sets. Her
personality had a certain distinction and charm . . . All this charm
is gone . . . For these thirteen years she has lived exclusively with
inferiors. Eight years in a small Australian town with all its
vulgarity and petty intrigues, five years in an Indian military station
consorting with clergy and Eurasians, and, above all, five years
servitude to a husband who is her inferior in every respect—a mere
elementary schoolteacher in training and a narrow evangelical prig
by constitution . . . She has practically fled from him. Poor clever
Carrie!

In August 1904 Beatrice gives an account of Dr Gore at Worcester
which reads like a scenario for an unwritten Trollope novel called *The
Bishop's Palace*. There are passages describing life in Whitechapel
which could come from one of Arthur Morrison's social novels, or the
tract-like fiction written by her cousin Margaret Harkness—who
introduced her both to the East End and to Sidney Webb. There are
accounts of a millionaire's drawing room and his country house which
read like Galsworthy or Bennett, 'a diligent master-craftsman' whom
she much admired; much that reminds one of Wells—after all, in *The
New Machiavelli*, he did turn the Webb story into a brilliant but
vindictive portrait—and more than one comedy of manners that falls
somewhere between Wilde and Barrie or Maugham.

For Beatrice had a theatrical sense as well, and her close friendship
with Shaw undoubtedly enhanced it. Here is a scene perfectly set for a
Shaw play. It was written in June 1896, when the Webbs were visiting
Bertrand and Alys Russell at Millhanger in Surrey. The other visitors
were the wealthy Bobby Phillimore, Sidney's running mate for the
LCC in Deptford, and his wife Lion.

A workman's cottage with stuffy attic bedrooms, but with the
inevitable decent size sitting room added on to it by the Russells . . .
A typical nineteenth century party—two aristocrats, married, one
to a charming American, the other to a bright talented Irish woman
(reputed a drunk Belfast carpenter's daughter who worked her way
up as a district visitor to Lady Henry Somerset's secretaryship,
from that to a seat on the St Pancras Vestry, and thence to a
marriage with her fellow vestryman—the socialist, philanthropic
and eccentric son of Sir Walter Phillimore). Both women a good
deal older than their young husbands, mere boys in age, though old

in thought and tasks. We six spent the Sunday lounging in the cottage garden, talking metaphysics, politics, very slightly interspersed with literature and art.

'Slightly interspersed with literature and art'. It is a telling and saddening phrase, which shows how Beatrice had already learned to displace her emotional energies from her private to her public concerns. By the end of the century, what she called 'the anodyne of work' had so deadened her imaginative impulses that she had lost interest in the undoubted literary skills that might have translated them into vigorous fiction. She had even begun to speak despairingly about the profession of letters and those who practice it—unless they put their skills at the service of what she called 'a living philosophy'. At the end of that road lay her senescent attachment to the 'new civilization' of Soviet Communism.

The trend was obvious soon after her marriage. Samuel Hynes, asking why the socialist movement 'which appealed to imaginative minds during the Edwardian period found no major literacy expression', was so struck by this philistine tone in Beatrice's diary that he squarely blamed the influential Webbs for the failure. They were, he wrote, 'persons without aesthetic sensibility . . . insofar as they understood literature all all, they saw it as an instrument of propaganda, a way of reaching large popular audiences, who were beneath the appeal of Fabian facts . . . they showed no sign of understanding what the literary imagination was, and their judgements on their friends' works were bleakly moralistic and utilitarian.'

I think that Hynes is too hard on Beatrice, for there are many regretful diary notes about art and literature over the years, and Sidney was the most prosy of men. But everything we know about the Webb partnership in mid-career seems to confirm that generally negative impression. Bertrand Russell, cycling through Normandy with the Webbs in 1903, complained that they always seemed to be measuring cathedrals rather than enjoying them. At Whitsun 1905, in one of the retrospects which she occasionally inserted, Beatrice admitted that much of their busy life was aesthetically bleak. 'What is utterly lacking is art, literature for its own sake, and music', she wrote—adding the revealing admission that Sidney was easily bored by such matters and by the kind of philosophical speculation that she found so appealing in Arthur Balfour. 'He prefers reading a statistical abstract or L.C.C. Agenda'. And in another of these frank admissions

Beatrice conceded that 'owing to our concentration on research, municipal administration and Fabian propaganda, we had neither the time nor the energy, nor yet the means, to listen to music and the drama, to brood over classical literature, ancient and modern . . . Such dim inklings as we had of these great human achievements reached us second-hand through our friendship with Bernard Shaw. Only our vision of the beautiful arose during our holiday wanderings, at home and overseas . . .'

When Beatrice writes about literature, moreover, we can see that Samuel Hynes is right in saying that her moralistic and utilitarian turns of mind made her a dullish critic. She liked the novels of George Eliot because they made her feel 'happier, more contented'. She found *Les Miserables* 'a glorious drama'. She disliked Balzac because 'his characters are corrupt' and he did not believe in 'the progress of human nature'. She annoyed Wells by praising the homiletic *War in the Air* instead of *Tono-Bungay*, which was his one serious attempt to match himself to James and Conrad. She also liked *Widowers' Houses*, which tried to put a Blue Book over the footlights, and found Shaw's plays about philandering distasteful. In 1910, after she had been to see *Misalliance* and then Granville-Barker's *Madras House*, she wondered 'whether these two supremely clever persons are not obsessed with the rabbit-warren aspect of human society'.

It is clear what kind of theatre Beatrice preferred. She thought Galsworthy's *Justice* 'great in its realistic form, great in its reserve and restraint, great in its quality of pity' and gave it what by 1910 had become the ultimate Webb seal of approval: 'its ideas all worked in with the philosophy of the Minority Report', she wrote. She even went so far as to applaud another dreary but well-intentioned play as 'the best thing yet written about life in a general mixed workhouse!'

This kind of priggishness grew worse after Beatrice married and as she grew older the conventional opinions of the Webb partnership became a matter of habit. In middle age she was affronted by Lawrence's 'sexual pathology' and found him devoid of art, humour and pure intellect. The 'promiscuous copulation' and 'chronic coldness' of the characters in *Point Counter-Point* filled her with 'simple disgust' and she repeatedly remarked on the utter absence of any kind of ethical code and of any fixed scale of values in the new novels she read in the post-war years. And this account of a weekend at Possfield Corner in February 1927 shows that there was no meetings of minds between her and Virginia Woolf, the one important writer besides Shaw and Wells with whom the Webbs were on visiting terms.

She is uninterested in politics, wholly literary, an accomplished critic of style and a clever artist in personal psychology, disliking the 'environmental' novel of late Victorian times, especially its latest exponent, Arnold Bennett. Like other work of the new school of novelists I do not find her work interesting outside its crafts-manship, which is excellent but *precieuse*. Her men and women don't interest me—they don't seem worth describing in such detail, and the mental climate in which they live seems strangely lacking in light, heat, visitibility and variety: it is a vast mist of insignificant and monotonous thoughts and feelings, with no predetermined aim, no powerful reactions from their mental environment—a curious impression of automatic existence when one state of mind follows another without any particular reason. To the aged Victorian this soullessness is depressing. Doubtless our insistence on a purpose, whether for the individual or the universe, appears to them a delusion, a pernicious delusion.

This is Beatrice at her most didactic, speaking in the tone of autocratic insensitiveness that Virginia Woolf disliked point-blank. 'In their efficiency and glibness one traces perfectly adjusted machinery', Virginia wrote of the Webbs after that same weekend, 'but talk by machinery does not charm, or suggest . . . it cuts the grass of the mind close at the roots'. For Beatrice—a creed-minded person as she herself conceded—did believe that there should be reasons for one state of mind (or one state of society) to follow another; and just over a year later, on 28th May 1928, she was reading *To the Lighthouse*, she was objecting to the stream of consciousness technique

because it assumes that the author *can* see into and describe another's mind and record what happens exactly as a person's behaviour can be watched, and his words recorded, and his sur-roundings and what happens to him retailed. What one suspects is that Virginia is telling you of her *own* stream of consciousness, the only one she knows of her own view and knowledge. And that brings me to the question. Could I record my own consciousness? So often it seems too vague and diverse and disconnected—there are cur-rents on currents, continuously rising and falling in relative vivid-ness, sometimes pictorial, sometimes vocal, sometimes aloof and detached, sometimes part of a pattern made up of personal contacts and relative positions, sometimes intellectual, concrete or abstract, or emotional personal or impersonal: all in all, even one's own consciousness defies description.

These two paragraphs do not show Beatrice at her best. Yet I find them fascinating—partly for their revealing, and restricting and characteristically Victorian insistence that art must have a purpose; partly because they show us very precisely the threshold between life and literature that Beatrice was never able to cross. I have been arguing that she had the necessary skills of a writer and more experience of life than most women of her time. But I feel she could never allow her imagination to organise her experience and that, I suppose, is the key to the whole business of the novelist. As she says, in effect, she could not even let her unconscious impulses run on without feeling that they would erupt into unmanageable gibberish, or perhaps, uncontrollable feelings which would remind her of the great crisis through which she had passed in the 1880s.

In that decade she lost her mother, and it took her years to come to terms with what she had lost; she lost the man whom she had loved to the point of desperation; and she lost her faith. I think that the acts of will required to hold her shattered personality together after these blows, and find both a creed and a career, exhausted her to the point of breakdown, even to the point of considering suicide—Beatrice says as much. I also think that this process of self-denial, this repression of family, sexual and religious feelings, must have driven all her imaginative powers into some ghetto of the mind where the 'Other Self' of the diary was confined. As her most profound emotions were mastered by her intellect, everything that touched upon things of the body, everything that might have given colour and joy and healthy vigour to her life, would have been subject to the relentless judgements and the kind of moralistic control that she gradually extended from herself to society at large.

I do not believe that Beatrice ever faced a conscious choice between art and socialism. I suspect that the denial of all the irregularities that art means to a talented individual preceded and prepared the way for Beatrice's conversion to the regularities of socialism.

Perhaps I can put it dramatically but simply. Beatrice Potter committed a form of psychic suicide when she denied her feelings for Joseph Chamberlain, and for the next fifty years she spoke only through the diary in which Beatrice Webb immured her. That was the voice, as Leonard Woolf once said, that spoke with 'the passion and imagination of an artist'—the voice of the novelist who might have been, but never was.

BOILING BELLOC

A. N. WILSON FRSL

Read 12th May 1983:
John Guest, FRSL, in the Chair

ALTHOUGH it is only thirty years since Hilaire Belloc died, he seems to belong to a past which is infinitely remote. When one hears his voice today, chanting the songs which he recorded in 1932 in those surprisingly high-pitched, reedy tones, it is almost as though we have heard the music of Tolkien's grey elves among the misty mountains. Tennyson's voice, crackly as the ancient cylinders make it sound, is more immediately modern: the voice of a man whom we can recognise as 'one of us'.

Belloc's voice is hauntingly odd: not merely because of its pitch; not merely because of the markedly Gallic accentuation of the letter 'R', but because it seems, rather as Ben Gunn's voice sounded on *Treasure Island*, the tones of a man who had not heard, or rather had not *listened to* another human voice for many decades.

The song on the disc which haunts me most is 'The Winged Horse', which he wrote in 1907 and which he framed initially within an odd little narrative, subsequently published in the volume *On Nothing* and entitled *On a Winged Horse and the Exile who Rode Him!* He encountered the exile when he was out riding on the Berkshire Downs, near the chalk White Horse of Uffington. The winged horse was a splendid creature which 'had all the strength of the horses of Normandy, all the lightness, grace, and subtlety of the horses of Barbary, all the conscious value of the horses that race for rich men, all the humour of old horses that have seen the world and will be disturbed by nothing'. The horse was grazing when the narrator encounters it. And 'the man who was the companion rather than the master of this charming animal sat upon a lump of turf singing gently to himself . . . ! He is staring out 'over the plain of Central England . . . He looked at it with a mixture of curiosity, of memory, and of desire which was very interesting but also a little pathetic to watch'. He tells the narrator that 'This kind of horse runs wild upon the heaths of morning and can be caught only by Exiles: and I am one' . . . He furthermore tells him that he has been long engaged in composing a great poem about the horse, but that so far he has only managed three verses. The narrator, in the best Chaucerian manner, is not a little scornful of the Exile's verses; and when the song has been sung, the stranger mounts the winged horse and they fly off over the crest of the hill vanishing from sight:

> It's ten years ago today you turned me out of doors
> To cut my feet on flinty lands and stumble down the shores
> And I thought about the all in all, and more than I could tell;
> But I caught a horse to ride upon and rode him very well.
> He had flame behind the eyes of him and wings upon his side—
> And I ride; and I ride!
>
> And once atop of Lambourn Down, towards the hill of Clere,
> I saw the host of heaven in rank and Michael with his spear
> And Turpin out of Gascony, and Charlemagne the lord,
> And Roland of the marshes with his hand upon his sword
> For fear he should have need of it: and forty more beside!
> And I ride: and I ride!
>
> For you that took the all in all, the things you left were three:
> A loud voice for singing, and keen Eyes to see,
> And a spouting well of joy within that never yet was dried!
> And I ride!

As a piece of writing, the whole essay, or story or episode is characteristic of the pretty, highly Edwardian manner which made subsequent generations feel justified in using the words 'belle-lettrist' as a term of abuse. It is, as the volume in which it appears is frank to own, 'On Nothing'; it is a doodle. The Mr Gradgrind in us wishes to point out that there are not such things as Winged Horses; that Belloc never met one; and that it was foolish to pretend that he did. The symbolist on the other hand, the admirer, perhaps of George Macdonald or C. S. Lewis, must be dissatisfied with the sketch for it is not whimsical enough. It leads nowhere. The exile appears, sings his song, and flies away. The narrator admits that 'there are no witnesses of the matter, and I go lonely, for many people will not believe, and those who do believe, believe too much'. It appeared originally as an item in a newspaper, the *Morning Post*; and it reads like the arrangement of a desk-drawer poem for cash.

Yet, while admitting that it is a doodle, are we not taught by many analysts of the human mind that doodles are pregnant with self revelation? I imagine myself in 1907 reading of this Exile whose eyes were 'a mixture of curiosity, of memory, and of desire which was very interesting but also a little pathetic to watch'. And I am looking at this date not at a man with a winged horse but at a man with a winged collar. And if that sentence has a very Chestertonian cadence, I make no apology, for the man in the winged collar is a more interesting and a more fantastical character than the man on the winged horse.

He is thirty-seven years old. His hair is cut short, *en brosse*. His eyes are deep set. They are very bright, and very satirical. He has a nose like a hawk's beak and a firm, thick set jaw and a mouth of which the upper lip is thin and stiff and the lower lip pouts and juts. The figure before me is not sitting forlornly on the turfy top of the Berkshire Downs, but on the Government Back Benches of the House of Commons. He is the Member of Parliament for South Salford in the Liberal interest.

It was one of the most remarkable parliaments in our history, not only because of the unparalleled liberal majority (377 Liberal seats, 157 Conservative, 53 Labour and 83 Irish nationalist) and not only because of the quasi-revolutionary nature of its measures and reforms; but also because of the extraordinary intellectual quality of its members.

Belloc, after only a year in the House had made a great name for himself. He had spoken on all manner of issues: on Ireland, on education, on South Africa, on the proposed new licensing laws, as well as on more private matters relating to his constituency. Moreover, he was, we are told from a contemporary report (in *Punch*) 'the most hard-worked of our younger Parliamentarians. The week-end brings him no respite from his labours, as he invariably spends it in the great heart of Salford among his constituents, where he conducts classes in military history, conversational French, and medieval theology.'

The wistful fantasy of an exile riding a winged horse seems, then, at first sight, an odd one for someone so deeply in the thick of things. But the man in the winged collar is not a fixed or sedentary creature. We are not to imagine him sitting placidly in the House of Commons during the week and doggedly in Salford from Friday until Monday. Unlike most members of parliament at this date, the member for South Salford had no income beyond what he could earn as a writer and a public speaker. His engagement diaries of the period are a ceaseless catalogue of public lectures, given for money, in places as far apart as Glasgow and Bristol, as Cheltenham and Chelmsford. The bibliography of his works informs us that during the four and half years for which he sat as a member for South Salford, he published 20 titles, which include three novels, a handful of travel-books and an extended and carefully mannered biography of Marie Antoinette, some 400 pages long, which some (though not I) believe to be his great work.

It is perhaps not surprising that with this wide range of demands on his time, he devoted little of his week to doing his 'job'. At this date he was literary editor of the *Morning Post*. We catch the flavour of his relationship with his employer and editor, Sir Fabian Ware in a note which is reprinted in Robert Speaight's biography:

Dear Belloc: I owe you an apology for the way I shouted at you this afternoon; but *please* don't on your rare and unexpected visits to the office (about which I shall say more on another occasion) stand in my door and wag a finger at me when I am engaged on private and difficult business. Yours FW.

The vignette is entirely characteristic and revealing. For although his life was crammed with manic activity, Belloc had a restless genius for wasting other people's time. He was always on the hoof and yet, deeply gregarious as he was, he had a compulsion to drag people along with him in his helter-skelter race through existence. He could never be still in one place. The wholly modern notion of 'relaxing' would have been alien to him. The wife of his great friend Cecil Chesterton (Gilbert's brother) would recall how, after an evening of shouting and drinking with his friends in El Vino or the Cheshire Cheese or in some Soho restaurant, Belloc would suddenly propose that they all went to France for a bit; 'and I have known them on occasions set off at a moment's notice without so much as a toothbrush and disappear into the void, *en route* perhaps for some interesting trees, whose acquaintance Belloc had made the previous summer in Britanny or the Pyrenees'.

As well as the bohemian life of Fleet Street which he enjoyed with the Chestertons and their coterie, Belloc also moved in what it was still proper to call High Society. If we form our impressions of Belloc entirely from G. K. Chesterton's accounts, we learn only of a man on the move between France and the Fleet Street bars; a poet, a controversialist, an apologist. We think of that composite and somewhat monstrous pantomime figure of George Bernard Shaw's creation, the Chesterbelloc. And there is no denying that this figure existed. But Belloc the tramp, Belloc the journalist, Belloc the Parliamentarian: these were only facets of his elephantine persona. The man in the winged collar, always sombrely dressed even before the great bereavement which overshadowed the second half of his life, was a figure cultivated by the most fashionable drawing-rooms of London. He was not a *parvenu*. His mother, Bessie Parkes, was the child of a prosperous Birmingham Liberal, Joseph Parkes, who had moved to London in the early decades of the 19th century and helped to found the Reform Club. Her father's house, subsequently the Stafford in Savile Row, was a building of palatial proportions where all the great figures in Victorian literary and political society would gather. Trollope, Thackeray, George Eliot, and Henry James were her intimates. There was nothing aristocratic about her; but she came from the very highest drawer of the *haute bourgeoisie*. The Parkeses were rich, and they were powerful. It is of no surprise to us then that nearly all Belloc's close friends, in early days, were also rich, or powerful, or aristocratic.

And yet—and here we begin to turn back from the man in the winged collar to the man on the winged horse—there runs through all Belloc's writings a feeling not merely of alienation from the rich world of Victorian and Edwardian High Society, but also a bitter hatred of it. On the one hand, we can observe that almost all his friends were drawn from the top rank of society: Lord Basil Blackwood, (who illustrated his early volumes of comic verse for children); Lord Stanley of Alderley (who sold him his beloved boat, the *Nona*); Lord Lucas, Lord Derby, George Wyndham, Evan Charteris, and Maurice Baring. On the other hand, as in his comic, so in his serious verse; as in his serious political writings, so in his satirical political novels, there is a strain not merely of violent radicalism, but of an almost obsessive hatred of the Rich.

We first set eyes upon the man in the winged collar in 1907, when as a comparatively new MP he still apparently believed that the Liberal government of Campbell-Bannerman, and subsequently that of H. H. Asquith would bring about a genuine change in English society. Within a couple of years, his political understanding had developed along two, apparently quite contradictory lines. On the one hand, he had come to believe that the House of Commons and parliamentary democracy itself was a sham; and that the two main parties, in apparent opposition to each other, were in fact in cahoots.

Asquith, far from wishing to push forward Lloyd George's radical Budget of 1909 through the Lords by threatening to create 500 peers was actually in league with the moneyed and landed interests, and with Arthur Balfour the Leader of the Opposition. Belloc, shouting himself hoarse in the hustings, claimed that what was needed was a revolutionary change by 'popular movement', and the abolition of the House of Peers. The reason for the failure of the revolution in the early months of 1910 was, quite simply, that all the powerful and rich men in England belonged to the same 'set'.

Arthur Balfour and H. H. Asquith might shout at each other across the floor of the House of Commons, but they attended the same house parties, shot the same grouse and tried to commit adultery with the same women. Moreover the front benches were peopled with men who were interconnected in the most intimate and familiar ways:

> We are not surprised at Romeo loving Juliet, though he is a Montague and she is a Capulet. But if we found in addition that Lady Capulet was by birth a Montague, that Lady Montague was the first cousin of old Capulet, that Mercutio was at once the nephew of a Capulet and the brother-in-law of a Montague, that Count Paris was related on his father's side to one house and on his mothers to the other, that Tybalt was Romeo's uncle's stepson and that the Friar who married Romeo and Julet was Juliet's uncle and Romeo's first cousin once removed, we should probably conclude that the feud between the two houses was being kept up mainly for the dramatic entertainment of the people of Verona.

And yet, although he had supported nearly all the measures of Lloyd George's Budget in 1909, it was not so much the collusion of the rich as the vulgarity of the radicals which appeared to offend him the most

about the Parliament which reassembled in his absence. He blamed
not merely the smart set and the 'Souls' for keeping up the farce of
Parliamentary government while actually governing by a clique. He
bemoaned the stinking corruption of that 'jumped up little Welsh
non-conformist' Lloyd George and regarded it as a sign of our collapse
as a civilisation that so few Members of Parliament could be found
from among the landed classes. 'The squires won't come', he moaned,
'all the experts will'. Parliamentarians, like Dons and the Rich, joined
the great company of men and women whom Belloc held in abomina-
tion.

I am not concerned today to enter into the question of how much
justice there was in Belloc's sense of the corruption that lay at the heart
of Edwardian political life. It is hard to see how his political career
would have developed had he thought otherwise.

He had no money and he had a very slender majority, cut in the
1910 election from a little over 800 to a little over 300. In all
probability, had he stood again at the end of that year, he would not
have got back to Westminster. I am more interested, however, in how
it all looked to him. Without quite recognising himself what he was
doing, he stacked the cards neatly against himself two different ways.
On the one hand, he was too radical to serve in the sham of a Liberal
Party led by Asquith. On the other hand, he was too much of a
gentleman to wish to have anything to do with a jumped up Welsh
nonconformist like Lloyd George. He was violently opposed to the
landed interest in the Lords. But he was apparently also of the belief
that the government of the country should be in the hands of those
who owned land and he complained that the 'squires' wouldn't come
down to Westminster. In other words, whatever happened in 1910,
Belloc was not merely going to leave politics (something which was in
any case a fait accompli). He was to be *driven out*. Like the exile who
rode the winged horse he is

> turned out of . . . doors
> To cut my feet on flinty lands and stumble down the shores,

a couplet of almost Swinburnian masochism. The song itself, penned
in 1907, claims that it was ten years ago today since this exile took
place; and in terms of Belloc's own personal biography that takes us to
the end of the year 1896, when he failed to be elected to a Fellowship of
All Soul's College, Oxford. Exactly as in his parliamentary career,
Belloc behaved in a way which would have made it impossible for the

fellows to elect him to their number. Suspecting, quite justly, an anti-Catholic prejudice in that institution, he placed a large statue of Our Lady on his desk while he was writing his examination papers. He was subsequently dined, as all potential candidates are; a nerve-racking occasion, when all aspirant prize-fellows are expected to be on their very best behaviour. Belloc, slightly older than the usual candidate, proud of himself for having been president of the Union and been placed in the first class in the Schools that summer, was not to be intimidated by a lot of dons. He stood in front of the fire and lectured to them about the superiority of the French army (in which he had served his year of national service) to that of the English. He bayed at them about troop movements, and harangued them about his lifelong obsession, 'the Anglo-Judaic alliance all over the world'. F. E. Smith, Belloc's great sparring partner in the Union walked away with him in the Oxford moonlight after this disastrous performance. Belloc was buoyant, confident that everyone had been impressed by the brilliance of his conversational powers. 'And do you think' Smith asked him, 'that you have improved your chances in that ancient house of learning?' Belloc turned to him and his cheerful expression turned to one of horror. It had never occurred to him, even though he had done everything to bring it about, that he would be rejected by All Souls.

This failure was not something to be shrugged off or lived down. It is not particularly disgraceful to fail the All Souls exam. Hundreds, like his contemporary John Buchan, have failed it without it warping their lives. But in the Belloc mythology this failure was magnified into Miltonic proportions, and in old age he would revert to it with tedious frequency. He revisited Oxford, for instance in October 1940 and recorded:

'It always renews my youth to see the bloody dons shuffling along the pavements of that town and stammering and yammering and talking to themselves as they go. Maurice Baring always says that it was God's Providence the Dons would not let me become a Don. But I deny this! If they had taken me in I should have turned them inside out and given them such Hell that they would have had to invent a post to get rid of me. Also, once I had the hall mark, I should hvae been able to expose their measly pretensions with authority. Writing, for instance, on the monstrous Elizabethan myth, leaving it a smouldering heap and signing the work H. Belloc, sometime fellow of All Souls'.

The most revealing phrase in this familiar rehearsal is 'once I had

the hall mark'. Belloc had an extraordinary strong sense of an official
world, an establishment from which he had been excluded. In middle
life, he felt he was denied any chance of political power by the
corruption of the parliamentary system. As a young man he was
denied status as an academic historian—'the hall mark'. And if it were
not for the fact that my last biographical work was a life of John
Milton, I should have felt strongly tempted to call my biography of
Belloc, on which I am currently engaged, *Paradise Lost*. For it was a
way of looking at the world which pervaded his entire imagination and
was wholly involuntary. The world was full of paradises from which
he had been excluded. I have already said that he mixed as an equal
with the rich and with the aristocracy. But he was not of their number.
The Parkes fortune, considerable as it had been, never came his way.
Part of his mother's inheritance was taken from her before his birth
when she became a Catholic. The rest was unwisely invested. And
although Bessie brought him up to believe that he was a man with
great expectations, Belloc was in fact a pauper. It should be of no
surprise, therefore that he charged about the world, aggressively
confident that it was populated with enemies, anti-catholic plutocrats,
scheming financiers, devious dons and corrupt politicians. One day in
1925, Maurice Baring had luncheon with Mrs Raymond Asquith,
Lady Diana Cooper and Belloc and the conversation fell to a trial
which was then being heard in the courts. Belloc knowingly said that
'They will arrange for this and that to happen', upon which Baring
exploded and said, 'For thirty years Hilary I have listened to that
nonsense of *they*? Who are *they*? On what invisible Olympus do they
sit?'

Baring's exasperation—put down by Belloc to the fact that his
friend was 'a good quarter jew'—was understandable. But it fails to
take account of how strongly Belloc was conditioned to believe in his
own personal myth as a Lost Paradise. On the very day of his birth, at
La Celle St Cloud outside Paris in the summer of 1870, the Prussian
armies had been poised to invade France. By the time he was a few
months old, they had reached Belloc's family home, smashed the
furniture, destroyed the family portraits and cut up the staircases for
firewood. His earliest pre-memories, the memories he was brought up
on, were of a perfect state which he had just missed, and from which
he had been excluded by a group of wicked people, in this case the
bloody bosche. Pass a couple of years, and we find another lost
Paradise. For when he was only two years old he was led by his

mother's hand as chief mourner at his father's funeral in the cemetery of La Celle St Cloud. It was only at the moment when the coffin was lowered into the ground that his mother turned his face away from the grave and clasped him to her own bosom.

The ruined French family home, destroyed by the Prussians; the lost father, taken from Belloc by whatever cruel fates govern the Universe; the lost fortune, mysteriously spirited away from his mother on the one hand by her anti-Catholic family on the other by the devious self-seeking of capitalists and financiers . . . We find before Belloc has reached the age of 18 that there are causes enough for his habit of regarding himself as an exile, an outsider, a man more sinned against than sinning, excluded by the world, the establishment, those in authority. 'Who are *they*?' we may ask, 'On what invisible Olympus do they sit?' Belloc would have been only too eloquent in his replies to such a question. And although I quote Maurice Baring's exasperation, I would not presume to a level of intimacy with Belloc which would entitle me to share it. I have drawn attention to a strain in his character which many of those who knew him have remarked to me, and many found abhorrent. It is not for me, as his biographer, to enter into such condemnations.

I feel, rather, as Carlyle's friend and biographer J. A. Froude who prefaced his great biography of the sage of Cheyne Row by acknowledging his subject's faults:

> Such faults as these were but as the vapours which hang about a mountain, inseparable from the nature of the man. They have to be told because without them his character cannot be understood, and because they affected others as well as himself. But they do not blemish the essential greatness of his character, and when he is fully known he will not be loved or admired the less because he had infirmities like the rest of us. Carlyle's was not the imperious grandeur which has risen superior to weakness and reigns cold and impassive in distant majesty. The fire in his soul burnt red to the end, and sparks flew from it which fell hot on those about him, not always pleasant, not always hitting the right spot or the right person; but it was pure fire notwithstanding, fire of genuine and noble passion, of genuine love for all that was good, and genuine indignation at what was mean or base or contemptible.

I suppose what I am saying is that Belloc had a very strong streak of irrational persecution mania in his make-up. I have already alluded to the rows he had with Sir Fabian Ware when he worked on the *Morning Post*, his failure to turn up at the office on any regular basis, and his refusal to do the work asked of him. Ware behaved with what seems commendable self-restraint. He went on paying Belloc, even when he failed to do the work; he did not lose his temper more often than was entirely natural. And yet, when Ware finally brought his Literary Editor's contract to an end, Belloc was convinced that he was being got rid of because he had 'attacked the Rich'. I think the best comment on this belief of his comes from Dr Rowse in his admirable essay 'In Justice to Belloc':

> In verse as in prose Belloc depicted Edwardian society, half carica-ture, half satire. Robert Speaight in his sympathetic biography, seemed to think that this put the old upper class against Belloc. Not a bit of it: they were his proper audience, they enjoyed him most. A mandarin society has a sense of humour and can laugh at itself and its denizens. (p. 77)

I think it is most important to see that; and to recognise that even in Belloc's assaults on the Rich there is a strong vein of irony. In fact it is hard to think of anything he wrote which is entirely devoid of irony. I want, in the remainder of this lecture to talk about the positive and imaginative uses to which he put the vision of himself as an exile, a wanderer, a stranger and a sojourner. I want to talk about him as a poet, as a story-teller, as an autobiographer, as the man of genius that I know him to have been.

But even as I do so, I feel his scornful eyes laughing at me for trying to chicken out of a discussion, however brief, of his role as a social prophet. *The New Yorker* cartoon which has most application to Belloc's position is the one whose caption reads: 'Just because I'm paranoid doesn't mean that people aren't getting at me'. We would however be here all night if I were to try to assess the extent to which Belloc was right about Dreyfus; right about exploitation of Chinese labour in the Transvaal or the influence of the great mining families of South Africa; whether he was right about the Marconi scandal, or about German casualty figures in the first two years of the Great War; or his Distributist Theory of economics could ever have been a practicable alternative to socialism as a way of demolishing the Capitalist menace.

I am more interested today in this ambivalent attitude to the society with which he was so intensely involved and concerned; and the way

that this attitude is put to the most potent imaginative use in his
art:

> The world's a stage. The trifling entrance fee
> Is paid (by proxy) to the registrar.
> The Orchestra is very loud and free
> But plays no music in particular.
>
> They do not print a programme, that I know.
> The cast is large. There isn't any plot.
> The acting of the piece is far below
> The very worst of modernistic rot.
>
> The only part about it I enjoy
> Is what was called in English the Foyay.
> There will I stand apart awhile and toy
> With thought, and set my cigarette alight;
> And then—without returning to the play—
> On with my coat and out into the night.

This *persona* of a lonely man, gazing at a bad play, but not feeling at
home in the theatre cannot be dismissed as a mere figment of poetic
imagination. In his restless crashing about the world, never still for a
moment, Belloc was actually like that, until the time when illness and
old age made it impossible for him to escape the Foyay. When he was
nearly 70, for example, the Hearst Press paid for him to go to Rome to
report on the conclave which resulted in the elevation of Pius XII to
the papacy. He was accompanied by Mr and Mrs Douglas Woodruff,
who arrived at the palatial hotel to find him standing restlessly among
the palm trees, the shimmying waiters, the glass tables and the
dowagers draped in fur: a scene which to Arnold Bennett or to Proust
would have been like a glimpse of paradise. 'My children', Mr Belloc
exclaimed, 'this is an anti-room to Hell. We must get out of here'; and
picking up his little Gladstone bag, he led them to a cheap pensione,
not of the cleanest, where he could eat bread and ham, and drink
cheap wine and smoke and shout and behave like the tramp he had
always been since he first began his peregrination through the world.
All Belloc's friends had stories like this to tell.

A high proportion of them belonged to that much maligned category, the Rich. All of them craved his company, besought him to stay in
their houses, eat their dinners, drink their champagne. And yet I
suppose that one of the best poems ever written about social life is

Belloc's Ballade of Hell and Mrs Roebeck. Few modern poems (with the possible exception of Larkin's

> My wife and I have asked a crowd of craps
> To come and waste their time and ours, perhaps
> You'd care to join us)

have ever captured the futility of social existence more vividly than

> I'm going out to dine at Grays'
> With Bertie Morden, Charles and Kit,
> And Manderley who never pays,
> And Jane who wins in spite of it,
> And Algernon who won't admit
> The truth about his curious hair
> And teeth that very nearly fit
> And Mrs Roebeck will be there.
>
> And then tomorrow someone says
> That someone else has made a hit
> In one of Mister Twister's plays,
> And off we go to yawn at it;
> And when its petered out we quit
> For number 20 Taunton Square
> And smoke, and drink, and dance a bit:—
> And Mrs Roebeck will be there.
>
> And so through each declining phase
> Of emptied effort, haded wit
> And day by day of London days
> Obscurely, more obscurely lit;
> Until the uncertain shadows flit
> Announcing to the shuddering air
> A Darkening and an end of it:—
> And Mrs Roebeck will be there.
>
> *Envoi*
> Prince, on their iron thrones they sit
> Impassible to our despair,
> The dreadful guardians of the Pit:—
> And Mrs Roebeck will be there.

I make no apology for quoting these poems in full because they are the essential complement of his serious prose works. *Contemptus mundi*, hard and black and funny and despondent lies at the very heart of Belloc. From it springs the stream of political novels culminating in 1928 with *But Soft We are observed!* in which the ultimate absurdity is achieved: a woman is made Prime Minister. From it, too, comes the lyricism of his three greatest prose works—*The Path to Rome*, *The Four Men* and the *Cruise of the Nona* in all of which, for most of the time, he is on his own, and happily so. In these prose works, too, he is at home in a way that he never quite seems to be as a figure in his poems. They are remarkably self-confident books. They are not essays or treatises with a definite shape. Once, when he was toiling across America, he wrote home to George Wyndham of his journey, and of the journey of life, 'Theology calls it a task. I call it a bloody ramble'. Those three splendid books are a bloody ramble. *The Cruise of the Nona* is the closest he ever came to writing a piece of straight autobiography. For the sea-journey from Holyhead round the coast of Wales and Cornwall and along the English Channel up to Sussex is really a frame for reflexion, and for memories of his meetings with his heroes: Jowett of Balliol, Cardinal Manning, and, one of the few twentieth century statesmen who inspired Belloc with any confidence, Benito Mussolini: 'What a contrast with the sly and shifty talk of your parliamentarian! What a sense of decision, of sincerity, of serving the nation, and of serving it towards a known end with a definite will! Meeting this man after talking to the parliamentarians in other countries was like meeting with some athletic friend of one's boyhood after an afternoon with racing touts or it was like coming upon good wine in a Pyrenean village after compulsory draughts of marsh water in the mosses of the moors above, during some long day's travel over the range' . . . Such were the thoughts which came to Mr Belloc in his boat when he had passed his fiftieth year, and the sea liberated him to say them. We need hardly remind ourselves that he was not alone, in 1924, in finding the Italian dictator admirable. Churchill, meeting him at about the same date, told Mussolini that he would be 'with him to the end of his struggle against the bestial appetites of Leninism'. Mahatma Ghandi regarded the Duce as a 'superman'; while the Archbishop of Canterbury of the day, Randall Davidson regarded him as 'the one giant figure in Europe'. The difference between these witnesses and Belloc is that they all came to forget that they had said such things, while he proudly went on proclaiming them until his hero was assassinated. I make the point purely as a temperamental one. Once he had arrived at an opinion Belloc liked sticking to it.

He was very well aware of the annoyance value of the last ditch.

In the *Cruise of the Nona*, he celebrated his life-long need of the sea. In *The Four Men*, a very much odder book, published in 1912 when he was 42, he celebrates Sussex. In this book, as well as the narrator, there are three other characters—a Sailor, a Poet and a world-weary old man called Grizzlebeard who join the figure called Myself in their journey from Robertsbridge deep into Sussex until they reach the narrator's own home, when

> The passer-by shall hear me still
> A boy that sings on Duncton Hill.

The Four Men are, of course, all Belloc himself. We have already seen him as a sailor and a poet. Even at the age of thirty when he first conceived of the book, or at forty when he wrote it out fully, he also saw himself as an old man. 'Ah! but if a man is part of and is rooted in one steadfast piece of earth, which has nourished him and given him his being, and if he can on his side lend it glory and do it service (I thought) it will be a friend to him for ever and he has outflanked Death in a way'.

When he really *was* a Grizzlebeard, and strangers would come to visit him at his house, King's Land, leading up their children to be presented, he liked to tease them by saying, 'My child, when you are old, you can boast that you once shook hands with Rudyard Kipling'. For Belloc, who liked to quote his old mother as saying of the British Empire, 'I hate the name and I hate the thing', there was something obviously and ludicrously inapposite about his confusion with the diminutive imperialist of Bateman's. In fact, there is something very similar about the way the two men idealised Sussex. For Belloc as a child, Sussex was the closest thing he ever had to a home. His mother, constantly flitting about between London and Paris, took a house at Slindon, near Chichester, a wooded old village on the edge of the Downs from where, if you climbed up beyond the houses, to Halnaker Hill, you could see the Channel. It was here that Belloc, as a very small boy, first had that sense of belonging to a place, that sense which he believed could outflank Death. And when he had married, and begotten children, it was inevitable that he should return to Sussex, where he bought the old mill and village shop at Shipley and created the legend of King's Land.

> If I ever become a rich man
> Or if ever I grow to be old,

> I will build a house with deep thatch
> To shelter me from the cold,
> And there shall the Sussex songs be sung
> And the story of Sussex told.

Belloc and his wife bought the place in 1906, just at the point when he was beginning his parliamentary career, and it remained his home until he died, some forty-seven years later. Here the exile who had been 'turned out of doors' by the dons of Oxford could find a home. And here the solitary man could be with his family and with the woman he loved. And here the pessimist could 'outflank death'. For three generations, King's Land was, indeed, a home to Belloc and his children and his grandchildren who grew up there. A great grandson still inhabits it. I have never visited a house which bore a stronger stamp of a man's personality, which was more pregnant with an atmosphere. Beside it, Abbotsford and Carlyle's House in Cheyne Row, both so heavily haunted by the fantasists who lived in them, are as devoid of feeling as an uninhabited modern flat. Every inch of King's Land is steeped with Belloc. The great hall, where village children would come to sing carols and be given their sixpences at Christmas, dominated by a huge lumpy staircase, a gift of Lord Astor which presumably once belonged to a house four times the size. So much for the grandeur of it. The entrance used by all visitors is not into the hall (never finished by the village builder) but through what used to be the old shop, still lined with the grocer's shelves and drawers and hung with scarlet silk damask, now faded to a palish grey. In this low ceilinged dark room the family would assemble; visitors would crowd in. And here the 'family gods', as old Bessie Parkes had called them, still stare down at you from the walls: white porcelain, medallions of Joseph Priestly and his friend Josiah Wedgwood; a cheap souvenir plaster bust of Dante, believed by every member of the family to this day to be a bronze; a portrait of Napoleon and, if it were holy week, some greasy French cards, depicting the fourteen stations of the cross and pinned up at random round the room, to be removed on Easter morning. The place struck different visitors in different ways. All who knew it well, even in its latter days, speak of it as a happy house, of its panelled dining-room as a place where you could rely on roaring good cheer, and on its mysterious chapel, off a half-landing on the first floor, as the core of all the laughter and the love of friends which the place embodied. To this day, it has a richly welcoming 'feel'. But it was not a place for the nice or the squeamish. I do not imagine that it was ever very clean, and no one would call it elegant. It is an architectural testimony to Belloc's restlessness. He was always adding doors and corridors. There is not a room on the ground floor, except his own study, which does not have at least two doors, one leading off to an unlit passage and another leading directly out of the house. It seems like the perfect stage set for a farce. Characters might at any moment intrude from left or right or upstage, banging their heads on lintels while the master of the house, even in this womb-like refuge could escape: 'on with my coat and out into the night'.

But the visitor he was most anxious to evade could not be outflanked by any number of escape routes. Belloc's wife had only six years of life at King's Land. He was forty-three, merely, and none of his children had grown up, when she died of an illness which was never satisfactorily diagnosed, in 1914. After this cataclysm in Belloc's life, from which he never recovered, King's Land began to grow its cobwebs and to take on some of the atmosphere of the enchanted palace in The Sleeping Beauty. The room where Elodie Belloc died was locked, never to be re-opened in Belloc's lifetime; and he never passed her door without kissing it or marking it with the sign of the cross.

I have spoken of Belloc both as a figure in his poetry and in life, as a cynic and a pessimist, hard done-by and exiled; standing on the edges of life now scoffing, now elegiac, or merely turning away from the farcical pageant of human existence. In his verse, he seems like a man who wishes to live without any saving illusions:

> The scenery is very much the best
> Of what the wretched drama has to show,
> Also the prompter happens to be dumb,
> We drink behind the scenes and pass a jest
> On all our folly; then, before we go
> Loud cries for Author . . . but he doesn't come.

I do not believe that a man who knew nothing of Belloc, and who read only these verses would begin to guess that he was chiefly regarded, in his lifetime, as an apologist for the Catholic religion. These poems of despair breathe no sense of redemption, no belief in the God of Love, no hope whatever of a resurrection to eternal life. But those who know a little more of Belloc will understand precisely that his temperamental pessimism, his hilarious frivolity and his ardent championship of the Catholic Faith are not at all incompatible; and that this last, his faith, is the very key to the man.

His most famous book, *The Path to Rome*, published at the turn of the century recounts a journey he made, on foot from Toul in the valley of the Moselle, to the Eternal City. Like the later books in which he is ambling through a place and letting his thoughts wander, *The Path to Rome* has almost no coherence beyond that given it by the *persona* of the author. Or so it would appear. It seems as if it is going to be a rather Stevensonian ramble on the model of *Travels with a Donkey*. And as though, for all the quaint figures he encounters along the way,

> The scenery is very much the best
> Of what the wretched drama has to show.

This is not so. We discover something else as the book develops. In England, Belloc is an exile. In Europe, watching the Swiss peasants going into Vespers, for instance, he is at home. *The Path to Rome* is a homecoming. It is a celebration of being European, of being Catholic. 'By the Lord!' he exclaims 'I begin to think this intimate religion as tragic as great love'. But it is a tragedy which he is unable to leave alone. He stands not outside, in the Foyay. Watching the peasants go into church, 'I put my cigar carefully down under a stone on the top of the wall and went in with them'.

The Catholic religion, the Catholic church, provided Belloc with that sense of home which was always lacking in his social and personal dealings. Whether he was travelling in the United States or in Poland or in Spain, the Catholic thing, as he called it, was always there. And Europe embodied it—for the Faith is Europe and Europe is the Faith. He never put his feelings about it more forcefully than when he wrote to Dean Inge: 'One thing in this world is different from all other. It has a personality and a force. It is recognised and (when recognised) most violently loved or hated. It is the Catholic Church. Within that household the human spirit has roof and hearth. Outside it, is the night:

> In hac urbe lux sollennis
> Ver aeternum, pax perennis
> Et aeterna gaudia.

I have probably already said enough to indicate why it was entirely in keeping with Belloc's nature that he should have adopted such a belligerent cheerfulness, a siege mentality towards all those benighted individuals outside the walls. There they all were, and none of them Catholics: the bloody dons ('on whom rests the curse of the Crucified God'), 'stammering and yammering'; the Protestants, with their naive belief in the literal truth of the Bible, which is, of course, 'a pack of lies'; 'lying as only shameless yids can lie'; Then there were the Jews themselves, 'poor darlings'—'guilty as hell', like Dreyfus or Sir Rufus Isaacs, bribing the sly and shifty parliamentarians to give them peerages. And who is this, hovering in the background? Poor little H. G. Wells, with his self-taught suburban values (he has not heard that 'the man who does not accept the faith writes himself down as suburban') preaching such lower middle class insular nonsense as Free Love, Socialism and Evolution.

> Noel, noel, noel, noel
> A Catholic tale have I to tell
> And a Christian song have I to sing
> While all the bells of Arundel ring . . .
>
> May all good fellows who here agree
> Drink audit ale in heaven with me.
> And may all my enemies go to hell
> Noel, noel, noel, noel.
> May all my enemies go to hell,
> Noel, noel.

There is not much evidence here of what Mr Auberon Waugh has lately described as the 'lovey-dove' element in Christianity, or what Belloc himself called 'the philosophy of good will to all men and being kind to the cat'.

Since this is the sort of Catholicism Belloc chose to present to the world, it is hardly surprising that 'when recognised' . . . it is 'most violently hated'. With his public self, Belloc would not have been happy if it were not hated. He had a compulsion to strike attitudes, and to adopt annoying poses, and to say deliberately and odiously provoking things. He was not the sort of religious apologist who, like C. S. Lewis a generation later, could bare his soul. Faith, as he knew very well, is the acceptance of things we do *not* know, rather than the giving of assent to readily verifiable notions. His own faith, as he confessed to his friend Gilbert Chesterton, was entirely a matter of the will. He was by nature a sceptic. He accepted the Faith as 'a thing,

not a theory. To you', he went on (Chesterton had just made his sub-
mission to the Catholic Church) 'who have the profound religious
emotion, this statement may seem too dessicate. It is indeed not enthusiastic.

It lacks meat. It is my misfortune. In youth I had it; even until
lately. Grief has drawn the juices from it. I am alone and unfed, the
more do I affirm the Sanctity, Unity, the Infallibility of the Catholic
Church. By my very isolation do I affirm it, as a man in a desert knows
that water is right for a man: or as a wounded dog, unable to walk, yet
knows the way home'.

It should not be supposed, however, that Belloc merely accepted
the *idea* of Catholicism as a great unifying European culture, while
privately rejecting its theological claims. This was the position of the
French journalist Charles Maurras, with whom Belloc is sometimes
compared. Nothing could be further from his position. Week by
week, day by day, Belloc knelt down and said his prayers. Whenever
possible, he heard mass, and as the years passed, his faith deepened
into an inner, secret thing which enabled him to accept his griefs and
disappointments. It would have been quite alien to his temper to make
any kind of parade of this 'private religion', but one entirely misses the
point of Belloc as a phenomenon if one disregards it.

In 1935, after an exhausting lecture tour in America, he made a sea
journey from Spain to the Holy Land, and from the Garden of
Gethsemane he wrote to one of his most intimate friends, Mrs
Raymond Asquith:

We are, of all our miseries, much the most afflicted by Mortality:
and that means not mere Death—the least of all our own, which
may be but a blessed sleep between the good troubled life and the
good untroubled life of beatitude—but the impermanence of all
things, even of love: the goodbyes and the changes that never halt
their damning succession: the unceasing tale of loss which wears
down all at last. *That* is mortality. That is the contradiction between
our native joy and our present realities which contrast is the Curse
of the Fall . . . [Death] is a curtain of Iron, a gulf impassable, an
impenetrable darkness, and a distance as it were limitless, infinite.
The miracle whereby such an enormity coming upon immortal
souls does not breed despair, is the chief miracle of the Incarnation
—and to work that miracle, the Incarnate—with what supreme
energy—accepted our pain, almost refused it but accepted it; and it

was greater than any pain of ours: physically beyond endurance and in the spirit a descent into Hell.

Now here is there meaning in prayer as at Gethsemane. Upon such a foundation perhaps the soul that prays shall lift into fulfill-ment and recovery. It is, that garden and its shrine, the very centre of man's world.

That was Belloc's Faith, and it would be an impertinence to comment upon it. He nourished it and practised it and fed upon it for all his grown-up life; and for all his public defences of The Catholic Thing, he was, though it would embarrass him most intensely if we knew it, obedient to the evangelical injunction to commune with God in the stillness and secrecy of his own heart.

Belloc, by the account of all his friends, was a deeply hilarious companion. You did not spend an evening in his company without laughing, without aching with laughter. His humour is thought by some to be brittle and superficial, a mere facade of barking laughter, hiding a profound inner blackness.

> I said to Heart, how goes it? Heart replied
> 'Right as a ribstone pippin'; but it lied.

Of course there is a sort of truth in this. Belloc set his heart on four things: academic position, wealth, political power and life with the woman he so passionately and romantically loved. All four things, by the time he had reached early middle age, had been snatched from him. And the first world war which followed almost immediately the death of his wife was to deprive him of many friends, and of his firstborn son. Moreover, whatever the reasons for promulgating his bizarre range of opinions, and whatever truth there was in them, his career as a satirist, a polemicist, an apologist, a journalist, earned him the bitter enmity of those who, at an earlier stage of life, could so easily have been milked and flattered and appeased. Since his death, he has suffered an absolute eclipse. Of his 150 or so published works, only a tiny handful are in print. His co-religionists, who for the last 20 years have been busily engaged in dismantling the Catholic thing which he fought so vigorously to promote, are for the most part ignorant that he existed, those who remember reading him in their youth (when they too believed that a vigorous Catholic leadership in Spain was prefer-able to an atheist soldiery who raped nuns and shot priests and forbade children to say their prayers) have rejected him with embarrassment. He has indeed, that lonely exile, cut his feet on stony lands and stumbled down the shores. Only the children still read him, and he makes them laugh and they go on laughing, about Lord Hippo and Lord Lucky for the rest of their lives.

Over the last few years, I have done little else except read and think about this exile in the winged collar who was 'very interesting but also a little pathetic to watch'. I have discovered that not all his opinions were silly. I do not think the world would be a worse place if the economy were ordered along the lines he expounds in *The Servile State*. And probably, if the western powers had taken heed of his book *The Jews*, published in 1922, there would have been no holocaust in Europe during the 1930s and 1940s and no wars today in the Middle East. He was one of the first English journalists to recognize the menace of Hitler: to see the implications of what Hitler was doing. Those last articles he wrote in the Sunday Times in 1941 when he reiterated that POLAND IS THE TEST—do not seem very wrong headed today. Forty years on, his words read like those of a prophet possessed of an infallible crystal ball. But he had the Cassandra touch and no one would listen to him.

I have gone through phases of being excited by his opinions; and longer phases of being simply exasperated by the casualness with which he never developed his thoughts. I have been bored to distraction by his potboiling repetitive histories of the Reformation. But my awareness increases day by day of a quality in Belloc which can only be described as greatness. His prodigious Napoleonic physical energy; his clowning; his prolific output of books; his preternatural eloquence; his gifts of prophecy and a fey sort of wizardry, an intuitiveness about human character (he was one quarter Irish) are only symptoms of the thing. He wasted all his powers. I do not think he was, in the strict sense of that word, a nice man. And one feels, with him as with Dr Johnson, that none of his published work quite matches the genius which was recognised by his friends in conversation. As some of those friends and his relations have recalled him to me, I have sometimes thought of Yeats's 'foolish, passionate man'. It seems a very lame way to end, but he was an original. He was utterly unlike any other human being who has ever trod the earth. He was the exile on the winged horse. And beneath the silly hats, and the vast black cloak and the even vaster black melancholy which shrouded his soul, there was 'a spouting well of joy within that never yet was dried'.

OSCAR WILDE AND LORD ALFRED DOUGLAS

H. MONTGOMERY HYDE D.Lit, FRSL

Read 7th October 1982:
The Earl of Longford, KG, in the Chair

I MUST begin, to use a parliamentary term, by declaring an interest in this subject. As an undergraduate at Oxford in the late nineteen-twenties I was by chance allotted the fine set of oak-panelled rooms on the kitchen staircase in Magdalen College which Oscar Wilde had occupied just fifty years earlier. Lord Alfred Douglas happened to hear from the editor of *The New Age*, a London weekly, that I had these rooms, and when I learned this I asked the editor that, should he see Douglas again, to let him know that I would be glad to entertain him in the rooms should he care to come to Oxford. The result was that Douglas wrote to me in May 1930 that he would very much like to do so, adding that he knew the rooms well since they had afterwards been occupied by his great friend Lord Encombe, son of the Earl of Eldon. 'I should like to see them and Magdalen again before I die!' he added. 'I have not been there for more than twenty years. I was asked a few months ago to make a speech or read a paper by the Oxford University Poetry Society and I more or less accepted but afterwards funked it and excused myself. Perhaps one day next month I might come down for the day if you would give me lunch?'

In a subsequent letter written a few weeks later Douglas told me that he had backed out of the Oxford Poetry Society's invitation because he had been asked to speak on the poetry of the nineties and he did not think he had 'any particular message' in this context. 'I do not consider that I belong to the "nineties" movement at all,' he went on. 'I always disliked and despised *The Yellow Book* and except Lionel Johnson, who was a great friend of mine, I did not admire very much any of the writers of that period . . . I hate reading my poems and in fact have never done it . . . I only made one speech in my life when I spoke about the Battle of Jutland and Winston Churchill for two hours at the Memorial Hall in Faringdon Street. The result was that I got six months imprisonment! But I discovered that I was a very good speaker which I didn't know before. I hope you have read my *Autobiography*?'

In place of Alfred Douglas the University Poetry Society invited Evan Morgan, later Lord Tredegar, to address its members. Incidentally, after he had succeeded to his father's Viscountcy, which he did in 1934, Evan Tredegar who was a Fellow of this Society for over twenty years, founded in his father's memory the lecture which I am privileged to give here this evening. In Oxford the Poetry Society asked me whether they could use my rooms as Evan Morgan wished to speak in them. I agreed and was also asked to be present although I did not belong to the Society. It was quite a large meeting and something like fifty members somehow crowded into the rooms to hear the speaker read his poems and talk on some aspects of modern verse, referring to Douglas and his poetry in the warmest terms and also to Oscar Wilde.

Since this is the Tredegar Memorial Lecture, perhaps I may be allowed to say a few words more about its founder, as he was interested in both Wilde and Douglas. Evan Frederic Morgan, second and last Viscount Tredegar, was an eccentric character, immensely rich, owning a turreted castle and 40,000 acres in Wales and another property near Dorking, where his mother lived; but he preferred to spend most of his time in Rosa Lewis's famous or should I say notorious Cavendish Hotel in Jermyn Street where he had the best suite in the house and the keys to all the secret doors. I was greatly impressed by his performance in the Oscar Wilde rooms. Afterwards I got to know him quite well, usually meeting him in the Cavendish where Rosa, being aware that I was poor and could not afford it, would put the champagne I drank on Evan's bill. He was a staunch Tory and a very pious Catholic; he held the office of Privy Chamberlain of Cape and Sword to two Popes, Benedict XV and Pius XI, and when on duty wore a romantic uniform with a plumed hat. He was also a great animal and bird lover; he had a pet macaw who terrified his friends and once pecked a black pearl ear-ring off an unsuspecting lady and dropped it in the fire. The last time I saw him was in March 1945 at Alfred Douglas's funeral at the Franciscan Friary in Crawley, to which he travelled down with me in the train from London and characteristically brought the largest wreath. Although he was twice married, he had no children by either wife and the Tredegar viscountcy became extinct with his death in 1949, although the Tredegar Barony and Baronetcy passed to an uncle.

In the event Lord Alfred Douglas never did come to Oxford for the proposed lunch, since after he wrote to me he went over to Paris to see his French publishers who were adding an additional chapter to his autobiography which does not appear in the English edition. While he was in Paris he became ill and had to go into hospital for an operation. By the time he had recovered and returned to England I was sitting my law finals in the Examination Schools and was consequently obliged to put off the lunch. However, after I had gone down I was to meet him for lunch at his house in Hove where he was then living with his mother the Dowager Lady Queensberry. On this occasion he spoke to me of his association and relations with Oscar Wilde fully and frankly.

Douglas, who was then sixty years old, began by showing me a letter he had received a few weeks previously, in April 1931, from Bernard Shaw. Here are some pertinent passages from it:

It is a pity that Wilde still tempts men to write lives of him. If ever there was a writer whose prayer to posterity might well have been 'Read my works; but leave my life alone' it was Oscar.

It is inevitable that you should appear in these biographies as a sort of *âme damnée* beside him, not in the least because you were a beautiful youth who seduced him into homosexuality (how enormously better for him if you had: you might have saved him from his wretched debaucheries with guttersnipes!) but because you were a lord and he was a snob. Judging from the suppressed part of *De Profundis* I should say that you did one another far more harm socially than you could have possibly wrought by any extremity of sexual affection. You had much better have been at the street corner with me, preaching Socialism.

However you need not worry. Your autobiography and your book *Oscar Wilde and Myself* anticipating the publication of *De*

Profundis in full (I have read both of them attentively) have made
your position quite clear; and you need not fear that any biographer
will be powerful enough to write you down.

. . . Your hatred of your father may have been very natural, and
richly deserved; but you were very young then; and if you had been
older, and unblinded by that passion, you would have made Oscar
ignore the card left at the Club as the act of a notorious lunatic lord,
and clear out before the police could be moved to proceed. Consequently we were all rather down on you at the time . . .

. . . That flowerlike sort of beauty must have been a terrible
handicap to you: it was probably Nature's reaction against the
ultra-hickory type in your father.

The card to which Shaw refers in this letter was, of course, the
gratuitously offensive one which Alfred Douglas's father Lord
Queensberry left at Wilde's club on 18 February 1895 with the words
'Oscar Wilde posing as a sodomite' scrawled across it, an action which
led Wilde to prosecute Queensberry for criminal libel with disastrous
consequences for himself after Queensberry had been acquitted.
Wilde's literary executor Robert Ross thought that the card had been
destroyed afterwards, and so did Wilde's son Vyvyan Holland who
had gathered this from Ross. However, some years ago, when the
Director of Public Prosecutions released the papers in the Queensberry case and they were placed in the Public Record Office, I discovered
the card there and had it photographed. It was marked Exhibit A and
is reproduced in my biography of Wilde and also in the later editions
of my account of the trials, as well as in my forthcoming *Annotated
Oscar Wilde* due to be published later this month.

Wilde and Douglas first met in the summer of 1891, at the end of
June or beginning of July. At this date Wilde was thirty-six and
Douglas a twenty-year-old Oxford undergraduate. Wilde was known
as the one-time leader of the so-called Aesthetic Movement, a poet,
short story writer and the author of a novel, *The Picture of Dorian
Gray*, as well as having edited a woman's magazine, *The Woman's
World*, for two years. He was also a potential dramatist, but none of
the three plays which he had so far written had been produced in
England, although the third one *Salomé*, which he had composed in
French specially for the French actress Sarah Bernhardt, was to be
banned by the Lord Chamberlain when in rehearsal because it
contravened the old rule against introducing Biblical characters on the

stage. Alfred Douglas, a Wykehamist, who had just completed his second year at Magdalen, was the third son of the ninth Marquess of Queensberry, the eccentric sporting peer nominally responsible for the rules of boxing, and a professed atheist, whose wife had divorced him for adultery and cruelty. The young Douglas was gifted with extraordinary good looks as well as poetic talents, shown by his early verse, and he was also something of an athlete since he had won the two mile race and the mile handicap in his college sports, as well as being a passable shot and rider to hounds. There was nothing at all effeminate about him. On the contrary he was quite masculine in character even if for a time he was bisexual. Indeed, shortly before he went up to Oxford in 1889, when he was eighteen, he was seduced in an hotel in the south of France by a woman at least twelve years older than himself, the divorced wife of an earl, which caused quite a sensation when his tutor discovered the liaison and promptly took him home to England. He has also admitted to having had sexual relations with another woman, even when his affair with Oscar Wilde was at its height. Incidentally Douglas had an allowance of £350 a year from his father, but this was stopped in 1893 when Douglas refused to discontinue his association with Wilde, and henceforward until he came into his inheritance of less than £15,000 on his father's death in 1900, he had no income apart from occasional sums and later a small allowance from his mother, who was a granddaughter of the first Lord Leconfield and had some money of her own.

Among Douglas's friends at Oxford was Lionel Johnson, an intemperate homosexual poet, and a Catholic convert, who already knew Wilde and had been at Winchester in Douglas's time. It was Johnson, destined to die a few years later as the result of his drinking habits, who introduced Douglas to the older man. Lionel Johnson called one afternoon in a hansom cab at the house in Cadogan Place, where Lady Queensberry was living with her son, whom she called Bosie, a contraction of 'Boysie' or little boy by which he had been known as a child. Johnson told Bosie that Oscar Wilde had invited them to tea at his house, 16 Tite Street, as the house was then numbered. They duly had tea in Wilde's book-lined study, on the ground floor, where there were also a few pictures including Aubrey Beardsley's drawing of the actress Mrs Patrick Campbell and also a plaster cast of the Hermes of Praxitiles. After tea during which they talked mostly generalities, though Wilde did most of the talking, he invited Douglas to lunch or dinner at his club. He then brought the

two guests to the drawing-room on the first floor and introduced them
to his wife Constance. 'I liked her and she liked me,' Douglas recalled
afterwards. 'She told me, about a year after I first met her, that she
liked me better than any of Oscar's other friends. She frequently came
to my mother's house . . . After the *débacle* I never saw her again, and
I do not doubt that Ross and others succeeded in poisoning her mind
against me, but up to the very last day of our acquaintance, we were
the best of friends.' At the same time honesty compelled Douglas to
admit that during the time he knew him Wilde was not very kind to his
wife. Theirs had been a love match and Wilde was still fond of her,
'but he was often impatient with her, and sometimes snubbed her, and
he resented, and showed that he resented, the attitude of slight
disapproval she often adopted towards him.'

On the other hand, what impressed Douglas about Wilde from the
beginning, as it did many others like Max Beerbohm, was the magical
quality of his conversation. 'I have never known anyone to come
anywhere near him,' Douglas told me, looking back some thirty years
after Wilde's death. 'He did succeed in weaving spells. One sat and
listened to him enthralled. It all appeared to be wisdom and power and
beauty and enchantment'. Or as Douglas put it in his sonnet *The Dead
Poet*:

> And as of old in music measureless
> I heard his golden voice, and marked him trace
> Under the common thing the hidden grace
> And conjure wonder out of emptiness,
> Till mean things put on Beauty
> And all The World was an enchanted place.

The friendship between the two men rapidly developed into infatuation on Wilde's part and Wilde made no secret of his feelings for
the younger man. 'He was continually asking me to lunch and dine
with him and sending me letters, notes and telegrams,' Douglas
subsequently admitted. 'He flattered me, gave me presents, and made
much of me in every way. He gave me copies of all his books, with
inscriptions in them. He wrote a sonnet to me, and gave it to me one
night in a restaurant. This was after I had known him about six
months.' The sonnet entitled *The New Remorse* was later published by
Douglas in 1892 in the Oxford undergraduate magazine *The Spirit
Lamp* when Douglas was the editor. Both Wilde and Douglas stayed
in each others houses and occasionally in hotels together and went for

trips abroad. Eventually, when Wilde was in Reading Gaol, he turned against his friend, and in the suppressed portion of *De Profundis* accused him of having made him waste his time: however the fact remains that Wilde wrote his best plays during the period of their association, whether it was in Babbacombe, Goring, London or Worthing.

On his side Douglas was completely captivated by Wilde's charm and spontaneous wit, of which Douglas gave me a good example. This was when Wilde remarked in the presence of a pompous schoolmaster and some other intensely earnest people that football was 'all very well as a game for rough girls' but it was 'not exactly suitable for delicate boys.' Douglas afterwards recalled that the effect of this innocent *jeu d'esprit* was quite devastating at the time, adding that he also remembered being rebuked for the unseemly laughter with which he greeted it.

In the end Douglas was without doubt more devoted to Wilde than the elder man had ever been to him. Nevertheless Douglas was also to turn against his friend after Arthur Ransome, better known as a writer of children's stories, wrote a critical study of Wilde, first published in 1912, in which he accused Douglas of having deserted Wilde when their brief reunion terminated following Wilde's release from prison; also after some of the suppressed parts of *De Profundis* charging Douglas with ingratitude had been read out in court during the libel action Douglas brought against Ransome in 1913, passages which (according to Douglas) he learned for the first time from Ransome's solicitors formed part of a letter which was addressed by Wilde to himself and which Ransome was to plead successfully by way of justification of his libel.

We must now consider the precise nature of the physical relations between the two men during their unfortunate friendship. In his autobiography, which originally appeared in 1929, shortly before I met him, Douglas confessed that for a short time there did occur between them certain 'familiarities' of the kind which not infrequently take place among boys at English public schools; but, he went on, 'of the sin which takes its name from one of the cities of the Plain there never was the slightest question. I give this as my solemn word before God, as I hope to be saved.'

In conversation with me some time afterwards Douglas enlarged on this theme, as he had done in a letter which he wrote to Wilde's biographer Frank Harris a few years previously. (I prefer to quote from this important unpublished letter which is now in the library of the University of Texas, as it gives Douglas's exact words.) He begins by admitting that when he first met Wilde he was not more innocent than any other boys of his age. He goes on:

> From the second time he saw me (when he gave me a copy of *Dorian Gray* which I took back with me to Oxford) he made 'overtures' to me. It was not till I had known him for at least six months, and after I had seen him over and over again and he had twice stayed with me in the rooms in High Street Oxford that I shared with my friend the late Lord Encombe, that I gave in to him. I did with him and allowed him to do with me just what was done among boys at Winchester and Oxford.
>
> It is hateful to me now to speak or write of such things, but I must be explicit. Sodomy never took place between us, nor was it thought or dreamt of. Wilde treated me as an older boy treats a younger one at school, and he added what was new to me and was not (as far as I know) known or practised among my contemporaries.

This was a species of oral homosexual intercourse which I feel that it is unnecessary for me to particularise. Douglas then continues:

> This happened the first time in his house in Tite Street after he had taken me out to dinner at the Savoy, a play (or music hall) and supper at the Lyric Club. I was staying in my mother's house in Cadogan Place, but my mother was away and there was no one in the house but the servants. Wilde was alone in Tite Street. I was filled up with drinks by the time I got back to his house about two o'clock in the morning. After about two hours discussion he induced me to stay the night in a spare bedroom and in the end he succeeded in doing what he had wanted to do ever since the first moment he saw me.
>
> Much as I was fascinated by Wilde and much as I really in the long run *adored* him and was 'crazy' about him, I *never* liked this part of the business. It was dead against all my sexual instincts which were all for youth and beauty and softness. After a time he tumbled to the fact that I didn't like it at all and only consented to it to oblige him, and he very soon 'cut it out' altogether. For at least six months before he went to prison no such thing happened between us, nor was it so much as hinted at after he came out two years later when I met him again.

Except in the case of Wilde I have never in my life had any immoral relations with a man older than myself. A little more than a year after Wilde's death I married. Such perverted instincts as I had disappeared completely as soon as I lost contact with Wilde and his *entourage*. If I had never met Wilde they might or not have disappeared sooner. As I said in cross-examination by Sir Douglas Hogg in my action against Northcliffe's paper the *Evening News* in 1922 (when I got a verdict and a thousand pounds damages), I did not 'grow up' till I was over thirty, and my 'perverted' period was simply a prolongation of my boyhood.

It is clear from this remarkable apologia that as a young man Douglas was bisexual. He admits that he always liked women and that he went with a woman before he met Wilde and often afterwards even when he was at the height of his friendship with him. 'I say this with no feeling but one of regret,' he adds. 'To me as a Catholic since 1911, all forms of immorality are now anathema'. Since 1913, when he separated from his wife, whom he married in 1902 although they continued to be on good terms, and I quote him again, 'I have lived a life of absolute chastity simply because of my religion, which I have accepted entirely and completely, tells me that any other state for me would be wrong.' In his opinion he felt that the fact of his prolonged chastity, being as it was against his inclinations, ought in fairness to be set against the fact that, as he puts it, he was 'occasionally immoral between the ages of twenty and thirty-two.' Finally he states that he would be willing to be examined by any number of doctors to disprove the charge of sodomy which was widely believed at the time. 'If I had ever allowed anyone (either Wilde or any single other person) to treat me in that way,' he concludes, 'surely a medical examination would reveal the fact.'

To me, this letter, corroborated by what he told me when we met, rings true, and I accept it as the truth. Like Wilde, Douglas was a pederast during his youthful years to which he refers. For example, in January 1895, when he and Wilde went to Algiers together, shortly before the production of *The Importance of Being Earnest*, Wilde wrote an amusing letter to Robert Ross, describing the delights provided for both himself and Douglas by the young local Arabs ('The Kabyle boys are quite lovely.') not to mention hashish. ('It is quite exquisite: Three puffs of smoke and then peace and love. Bosie wakes up at night and cries like a child for the best hashish.') This letter, which belonged to the late Lord Queensberry, is not reproduced in either of Sir Rupert Hart-Davis's editions of Wilde's letters, but the complete text appears in my biography of Wilde.

There are in particular two questions which require examination in the context of the Wilde–Douglas affair. The first is the statement, which Douglas has made over and over again in his later writings, that Wilde's leading counsel Sir Edward Clarke promised during the consultations with Wilde and his solicitors and the other counsel, at which Douglas claims to have been present, to call Douglas as a witness in the first trial immediately after Clarke had made his opening speech to the jury. Douglas asserts that by changing his mind and not doing so, Clarke deliberately broke his promise. Wilde's version of the matter was contained in the letter which he sent to the *Evening News* and which appeared in the afternoon editions on the same day as Wilde withdrew from his prosecution of Queensberry and Queensberry was acquitted. The letter, which incidentally was drafted by Ross although signed by Wilde, began by stating that it would have been impossible for Wilde to prove his case without putting Douglas in the witness box against his father. 'Lord Alfred Douglas was extremely anxious to go into the box, but I would not let him do so,' Wilde's letter continued. 'Rather than put him in so painful a position, I determined to retire from the case, and to bear on my own shoulders whatever ignominy and shame might result from my prosecuting Lord Queensberry.'

In fact this letter is as misleading as Douglas's charge against Sir Edward Clarke is without foundation or at best based on a misunderstanding of what Clarke actually said at the consultation in his chambers when Douglas offered to testify against his father. 'There is not a fragment of truth in any of these statements,' wrote Clarke afterwards. 'The question of Lord Queensberry's character was quite irrelevant to the case, and if an attempt had been made to give such evidence the judge would of course have peremptorily stopped it.' This has been confirmed by the late Sir Travers Humphreys, the well known criminal judge, who was a junior counsel in the trial and the two which followed it and who wrote in the foreword which he contributed to my edition of the trials: 'There was no admissible evidence which Douglas could have given, since the issue was not concerned with the treatment of his family by the Marquess, but simply—was it true that Wilde had posed as alleged?'

Nor was the reason for Wilde's withdrawal from the Queensberry prosecution what he stated in his letter to the *Evening News*. The real reason was as stated in Clarke's unpublished recollections of the trial:

When I saw Mr Wilde, I told him that it was impossible in all the circumstances to induce a jury to convict of a criminal offence a father who was endeavouring to save his son from what he believed to be an evil companionship. I said that upon full consideration I advised him in his own interest to allow me to make that statement to the Court and to withdraw from the prosecution; and I said that, if the case went to its end and the jury found that the accusations were justified [these were the accusations of immorality with named youths in Queensberry's plea of justification] the judge would unquestionably order his arrest. He listened quietly and gravely, and then thanked me for my advice and said he was prepared to act upon it. I then told him that there was no need for his presence in Court while the announcement was being made. I hoped and expected that he would take the opportunity of escaping from the country, and I believe he would have found no difficulty in doing so.

Douglas was present throughout these proceedings, but after Wilde's arrest and before Wilde took Queensberry's place in the dock at the Old Bailey, Sir Edward Clarke with his client's assent persuaded Douglas to leave the country on the grounds that his continued presence would prejudice Wilde's chances of acquittal. Accordingly Douglas crossed over to France where he stayed in Dieppe, Paris and Rouen and where he again offered to give evidence for Wilde. He telegraphed in this sense to Clarke, only to receive a severe rebuke from Wilde's solicitors, who informed him that his telegram was most improper and adjured him not to attempt any further interference, which, in the solicitors' words 'can only have the effect of rendering Sir Edward's task still harder than it is already.'

After the jury had failed to agree at the first trial and Wilde was released on bail, Douglas thought that his friend was almost certain to be found not guilty the second time. On 15 May 1895, Douglas wrote to 'my darling Oscar' from the Hotel des Deux Mondes in Paris where they had often stayed together in the past: 'Have just arrived here. It seems too dreadful to be here without you, and I hope you will join me next week . . . The proprietor is very nice and *most* sympathetic, he asked after you at once and expressed his regret and indignation at the treatment you had received.' The news of Wilde's conviction, which

Douglas received ten days later, came as a stunning blow. Never-theless he expressed his appreciation in the warmest terms to Clarke for his performance in court where he defended Wilde with-out fee.

'You will forgive me I am sure for writing to you now,' Douglas wrote to Clarke next day from Rouen 'to thank you from the bottom of my heart for your noble, generous and superb efforts on behalf of my friend. It seems almost an impertinence from one so miserable as myself, so broken in heart and spirit, so defamed and ruined to offer you my poor gratitude, but believe me I shall never cease to think of you with the profoundest gratitude and admiration. That you were unable to get a verdict seems to me, a layman, a piece of monstrous injustice, and the sentence was worse than I would have thought possible after the first disagreement.' Nothing here, you will note, about Clarke having originally promised to call Douglas as a witness and having failed to do so then and in the two subsequent trials. Nor is there anything but praise for Clarke by Douglas in his book *Oscar Wilde and Myself* (1914). It was not until his later works, the two editions of his *Autobiography* (1929 and 1931), his autobiographical work *Without Apology* (1938) and *Oscar Wilde: A Summing Up* (1939), as well as what he told me at our first meeting in 1931, that he rounded on Clarke and declared that he had broken his word to put him in the witness box and so let down his client. Clarke was a ruffian thinking only of his reputation at the Bar, Douglas told me. This, of course, is absolute nonsense. Clarke's performance in all three trials was out-standingly able, and what is more, as I have said, he defended Wilde in both his trials free of charge.

On the other hand, because Wilde was proved to have been on terms of criminal intimacy with a number of named youths, Douglas was widely assumed to have been on similar terms with Wilde, if not actually an accomplice, as evidenced by the two particularly affection-ate letters from Wilde to Douglas introduced at the trials, as well as Douglas's lyric *Two Loves* and his sonnet *In Praise of Shame* which appeared in December 1894 in the first and only issue of the unfortun-ate undergraduate magazine *The Chameleon*, to which Wilde contri-buted his *Phrases and Philosophies for the Use of the Young*, and on all of which Wilde was cross-examined in the trials.

The last twelve lines of Douglas's *Two Loves*, which he wrote in September 1892, read:

'Sweet youth,
Tell my why, sad and sighing, dost thou rove
These pleasant realms? I pray thee tell me sooth
What is thy name?' He said: 'My name is Love,'
Then straight the first did turn himself to me,
And cried: 'He lieth for his name is Shame.
But I am love, and I was wont to be
Alone in this fair garden, till he came
Unasked by night; I am true Love, I fill
The hearts of boy and girl with mutual flame.'
Then sighing said the other, 'Have your will,
I am the Love that dare not speak its name.'

Questioned about this poem by Charles Gill, who led the prosecution in Wilde's first trial, Wilde denied that the love described related to natural and unnatural love. Gill thereupon asked, 'What is the "Love that dare not speak its name"?'
Wilde replied:

'The love that dare not speak its name' in this century is such a great affection of an elder for a younger man as there was between David and Jonathan, such as Plato made the very basis of his philosophy, and such as you find in the sonnets of Michelangelo and Shakespeare. It is that deep, spiritual affection that is as pure as it is perfect. It dictates and pervades great works of art like those of Shakespeare and Michelangelo, and those two letters of mine, such as they are. It is in this century misunderstood, so much misunderstood that it may be described as the 'Love that dare not speak its name', and on account of it I am placed where I am now. It is beautiful, it is fine, it is the noblest form of affection. There is nothing unnatural about it. It is intellectual, and it repeatedly exists between an elder and a younger man, when the elder has intellect, and the younger man has all the joy, hope, and glamour of life before him. That it should be so, the world does not understand. The world mocks at it and sometimes puts one in the pillory for it.

Wilde's words produced a spontaneous outburst of applause from the public gallery, mingled with some hisses, which moved the judge to say that he would have the Court cleared if there was any further manifestation of feeling. Max Beerbohm, who was present, told me when I met him many years later, that he had never heard anything like it. It was certainly a remarkable impromptu performance on Wilde's part.

In the last trial the foreman of the jury interrupted Mr Justice Wills's summing up and asked the judge whether in view of his intimacy with the accused man a warrant was ever issued for the apprehension of Lord Alfred Douglas. 'I should think not,' the judge replied, adding in answer to further questions that a warrant would not be issued without evidence of some fact, of something more than intimacy. 'You must remember,' the judge went on, 'that no prosecution would be possible on the mere production of Mr Wilde's letters to Lord Alfred Douglas. Lord Alfred Douglas, as you know, went to Paris at the request of the defendant, and there he has stayed, and I know absolutely nothing more about him. I am as ignorant in this respect as you are. It may be that there is no evidence against Lord Alfred Douglas. But about that I know nothing. It is a thing we cannot discuss.' At the same time, Mr Justice Wills told the jury—and I quote his exact words—'I believe that to be the recipient of such letters and to continue the intimacy is as fatal to the reputation of the recipient as to the sender, but you have really nothing to do with that at present,' adding that the supposition that Douglas would be spared because he was Lord Alfred Douglas was one of the wildest injustice. 'The thing is utterly and hopelessly impossible!' the judge declared.

Douglas was still in France when Wilde was released from prison in May 1897. He immediately wrote to Wilde who invited him to stay at the chalet he had taken at Berneval near Dieppe; but a few days later, in June 1897, Wilde received a letter from his solicitor to the effect that Queensberry was having him watched and would certainly intervene and create a fresh scandal if he discovered that his son was there, so that Wilde telegraphed Douglas putting him off, but at the same time, as Douglas put it, 'he declared his devotion to me was only enhanced by our continued separation.' Eventually they met at Wilde's suggestion in Rouen at the end of August in what was a happy but tearful reunion. 'Poor Oscar cried when I met him at the station,' Douglas recalled later. 'We walked about all day arm in arm, or hand in hand, and were perfectly happy.' They agreed to meet in Naples, about six weeks later. Meanwhile Douglas's mother and his sister Edith came to France to take the waters at Aix-les-Bains, where Bosie joined them. It was while he was there, on 20 September 1897, that he wrote to Wilde in a hitherto unpublished letter on the subject of his returning to England. Douglas had evidently been afraid to make this move before, fearing possible arrest, but he now wished to go back to arrange for the publication of some of his poems. He had learned from his cousin, George Wyndham, that Mr Asquith, who had been Home Secretary at the time of the Wilde trials, had written saying that no steps had ever been taken against Douglas by the Director of Public Prosecutions, Hamilton Cuffe, and that, as it was impossible for anything fresh to have occurred since he left England, it was obvious that there was nothing to prevent his return. 'It is quite official information,' wrote Douglas. 'However on the top of this, Cuffe, the public prosecutor, has written to my uncle George Finch [his cousin] saying that he hears that I think of coming back and that he thinks it would be very *inadvisable*, so it is very contradictory. It was all settled that I should go to Clouds, a party had been got up there to meet me, and now it is all off. My mother is going to see Cuffe personally.' Clouds was the Wiltshire home of Lady Queensberry's uncle Percy Scawen Wyndham and his wife Madeline who had frequent house parties there. In the event Douglas did not go back to England until November 1898, fourteen months later.

Meanwhile, in September 1897, he joined Wilde in the train from Aix-les-Bains to Naples, where they took a villa at Posilippo. During the time they spent there Wilde revised and added to *The Ballad of Reading Gaol*, while Douglas composed some poetry. 'Bosie has written three lovely sonnets which I have called the *Triad of the Moon*' Wilde wrote to Robert Ross on 1st October 1897—'they are quite wonderful.' Afterwards Douglas remarked in his autobiography: 'I had forgotten till I read this letter that it was Oscar who gave me the name *Triad of the Moon* for my three sonnets . . . In view of Wilde's contemptuous remarks about my "undergraduate verse", made when he was in a rage and quoted by [Frank] Harris, I am glad to have this independent evidence that he did not always despise my poetry.' The sonnets were published anonymously in Douglas's *The City of the Soul* two years afterwards and subsequently republished on several occasions under Douglas's name. For his part Douglas had no objection to Wilde's borrowing two lines from another of Douglas's sonnets for *The Ballad*, and he also persuaded Wilde to overrule Robert Ross's objection to the phrase 'the man in red who reads the law' and also to Ross's suggestion that the last twenty stanzas should be omitted, that is from the point where the propaganda against capital punishment which Wilde desired to make begins. 'It was I again who influenced him here', Douglas stated afterwards. 'If the poem had ended at the point suggested by Ross it would have been a heavy loss to literature.'

After Wilde and Douglas were obliged to part company in December 1897, when Constance threatened to stop the allowance of £3 a week she was making him, Wilde wrote to Robert Ross that—and I quote—'as soon as there was no money left Bosie left me', describing Douglas's departure as 'the most bitter experience of a bitter life.' This charge was untrue and unfair since before he left Douglas gave Wilde £200, which Douglas had got from his mother Lady Queensberry, together with the money to pay their hotel bill in Naples before they moved into the villa at Posilippo. Shortly afterwards Wilde wrote to Ross in an undated and unpublished letter, formerly in the collection of the late Lord Queensberry: 'The idea for the *Ballad* came to me while I was in the dock waiting for my sentence to be pronounced. Bosie must not say that he originated it.' In fact Douglas never said anything of the kind. As he put it afterwards, apart from the sonnet to which one passage in the *Ballad* owed something, 'I do not for a moment claim that I helped Wilde to write this great poem.'

Douglas's first volume of poems to be published in England came out in the autumn of 1898, under the pseudonym 'A Belgian Hare'. It was an amusingly illustrated collection of nonsense verse about animals for children called *Tails with a Twist*, and was published by Edward Arnold, who bought the copyright outright for £50. Many years later when Douglas told Bernard Shaw what he had done, Shaw gave him a valuable piece of advice: 'Never, on your life, part with a copyright. Always hold on to it, and *licence* publication or performance.' Bosie's second book of poems to appear in England *The City of the Soul* was published anonymously under the imprint of Grant Richards in the early summer of 1899. By this time Douglas was back in Paris and Wilde was dining with him in his apartment in the Avenue Klèber when the first review, in *The Outlook*, arrived. It was a glowing one headed 'A Great Unknown'. Though anonymous, it had in fact been written by Lionel Johnson, who may well have guessed the author's identity as that of his old Oxford friend, since he announced: 'Among crowds of clever versifiers here comes a poet!'

This was one of Wilde's intermittent meetings with Douglas, whom on another occasion he accused of being narrow and mean—'Boys, brandy and betting monopolise his soul,' Wilde wrote to Ross in June 1900. 'He is really a miser: but his method of hoarding is spending: a new type.' Yet after Douglas's father had died at the beginning of that year, Douglas gave Wilde the best part of £400, as proved by the entries in his bank account, and he also paid Wilde's funeral expenses, although Ross did not warn Douglas of the seriousness of Wilde's illness until it was too late, and by the time Douglas arrived in Paris for the funeral Ross had been through Wilde's effects and taken possession of a number of Douglas's letters to Wilde which he found among them and subsequently retained, as he did the *De Profundis* manuscript. In fact, only three of Douglas's letters to Wilde are known to have survived; they are in the William Andrews Clark Memorial Library in the University of California, Los Angeles. As for the *De Profundis* manuscript this was deposited by Wilde's literary executor Robert Ross in the British Museum, now the British Library, in the latter part of the year 1909 on condition that it should remain sealed up for fifty years, when presumably everyone mentioned in it, including Douglas to whom it was addressed, would be dead, and that it should not be opened to the public until the 1st January 1960. Except that at Ross's instigation it was produced by the Museum director in court during the libel action which Douglas brought against Arthur Ransome in 1913, this condition was fulfilled. A few minutes after ten o'clock on the morning of January 1st I presented myself at the manuscript department of the Museum and was thus the first member of the public to be allowed to examine it.

I have already dealt with the reasons why Sir Edward Clarke, Wilde's leading counsel in the trials, could not call Douglas as a witness, although Douglas was most anxious to testify. I now come to the other matter of particular importance—what actually happened over Wilde's *De Profundis* letter to Douglas and why Douglas never received the original of what must surely be the longest letter in epistolary history, over 60,000 words.

In this letter, which begins 'Dear Bosie' and ends 'Your affectionate friend Oscar Wilde', Wilde reproached Douglas for his conduct during their ill-fated friendship before Wilde's downfall; also for the fact that while he was in prison Douglas had not written him a single line, that Douglas had proposed to publish the letters he had received from Wilde, while Wilde was in Holloway Prison awaiting trial, in the French journal *Mercure de France* and that Douglas wished to dedicate to Wilde the first collection of his poems which the same journal was publishing. In the event the letters were not published and Douglas's poems appeared in 1896 without any dedication. Wilde was not allowed by the prison authorities to send the *De Profundis* letter to Robert Ross for onward transmission to Douglas when he had finished it in March 1897, but he was given permission to take it out with him on his release. But he was allowed to send Ross the letter dated 1st April 1897 with his instructions to Ross to have two complete copies made of the *De Profundis* manuscript, one for Ross and the other for himself, also extracts for two of his women friends Adela Schuster, who had given Wilde £1,000 at the time of his trials, and Frances Forbes-Robertson, sister of the well-known English actor-manager Sir Johnston Forbes-Robertson. 'I know both these sweet women will be interested to know something of what is happening to my soul,' Wilde wrote in his letter to Ross—'not in the theological sense, but merely in the sense of the spiritual consciousness that is separate from the actual occupations of the body.'

Wilde's instructions were explicit:

As regards the mode of copying [he wrote] . . . I think the only thing to do is to be thoroughly modern, and to have it typewritten. Of course the manuscript should not pass out of your control, but could you not get Mrs Marshall to send down one of her type-writing girls—women are the most reliable, as they have no memory for the important—to Hornton Street or Phillimore Gardens to do it under your supervision? I assure you that the type-writing machine, when played with expression, is not more annoying than the piano when played by a sister or near relation. Indeed many, among those most devoted to domesticity, prefer it.

Perhaps I should explain that Mrs Marshall ran a typewriting agency which had typed the acting versions of Wilde's plays, and that Wilde's friends More Adey and Robert Ross lived respectively in Hornton Street, Kensington, and nearby Upper Phillimore Gardens.

Wilde's instructions continue:

The copy done and verified from the manuscript, the original should be despatched to A[lfred] D[ouglas] by More [Adey], and another copy done by the typewriter so that *you* should have a copy as well as myself.

If the copying is done at Hornton Street the lady type-writer might be fed through a lattice in the door like the Cardinals when they elect a Pope, till she comes out on the balcony and can say to the world '*Habet Mundus Epistolam*' for indeed it is an Encyclical Letter, and as the Bulls of the Holy Father are named from their opening words, it can be spoken of as the *Epistola: In Carcere et Vinculis*.

There is no need to tell A[lfred] D[ouglas] that a copy has been taken unless he should write and complain of injustice or misrepresentation in the letter: then he should be told that a copy has been taken. I earnestly hope the letter will do him good. (It is the first time anyone has ever told him the truth about himself . . . I hope someone will let him know that the letter is one he thoroughly deserves, and that if it is unjust, he thoroughly deserves injustice.)

Wilde was released from prison on 19 May 1897 and crossed the same evening by the night boat to Dieppe where Robert Ross and Reggie Turner, another friend, met him at the quay side. According to Ross, Wilde was holding in his hand a large sealed envelope which he gave Ross after he had landed. 'This, my dear Robbie, is the great manuscript about which you know,' he said. The manuscript was of course *De Profundis*. In his many subsequent written communications with Ross, Wilde only alluded to it on two occasions. One was in a postcard from Berneval dated 15th June 1897, complaining that Ross had never told him anything about the manuscript or the copying. 'Pray let there be no further conspiracies,' he added. 'I feel apprehensive. It is only by people writing to me the worst that I can know the best.' The second allusion is to the possibility of a third typescript being made by a friend of Ross's called Dixon, who lived some distance from London. 'I don't think I would like the type-written manuscript sent to him,' Wilde wrote to Ross a few weeks later on 20 July. 'It might be dangerous. Better to have it done in London, scratching out Bosie's name, mine at the close, and the address. Mrs Marshall can be relied upon.' It seems possible that Mrs Marshall's typewriting agency made this third typescript, for what purpose is not known. What *is* known is that Ross did not send the original manuscript to Douglas but one of the typed copies, the top one, although Douglas always denied having received it. The second copy, a carbon, was retained by Ross and bequeathed by him at his death in 1918 to Wilde's younger surviving son Vyvyan Holland. In 1949, Mr Holland published what he claimed to be 'the first complete and accurate version' of the whole of *De Profundis* from this carbon copy. In fact it was not complete, lacking about a thousand words, as appears from the version based on the manuscript and first published by Sir Rupert Hart-Davis in his admirable edition of Wilde's letters published in 1962. Nor was it accurate since it contained numerous errors and misprints probably caused by Ross dictating it to a typist who misheard or misunderstood him. As regards the third typescript, about which Wilde wrote, assuming that it was made, this may be the one at present in the possession of Mrs Alison Augustin of Menlo Park, California.

We also know that as early as February 1897, when Wilde was still at Reading, Douglas had been warned by More Adey to expect a letter from Wilde. 'I look forward without much excitement to Oscar's letter,' Douglas replied to Adey on the 8th of that month. 'If he is going to abuse me I would rather not see it . . . Please let me know if possible by return when exactly I may expect his letter.' Adey's reply has not survived but presumably it was to the effect that Douglas would get it if and when Wilde was allowed to send it.

According to a statement by Ross, now in the Clark Library, one of the typed copies was sent by him to Douglas on 9 August 1897 and its receipt acknowledged by him. Also in a letter from Douglas to More Adey written from Nogent-sur-Marne on 30 June 1897, Douglas declared that he had just received an 'enormous envelope' from Ross, which turned out to be what was, to quote Douglas, a 'typewritten statement', to which Ross had referred in a previous letter. This may well have been the *De Profundis* copy, although as I have said Ross has stated that it was not despatched until some weeks later. At all events Douglas has admitted to reading a few pages of Ross's typescript and then tearing up the whole document in a rage and throwing the fragments into the river Marne. It is clear that, when he did so, assuming that the document was the *De Profundis* copy, he had not read as far as the published portions, since he would unquestionably have recognised them when the first published version, edited by Ross, appeared in 1905. Nor is it conceivable that he would have reviewed the work, as he did at the time of its publication in the journal *Motorist and Traveller* on 1 March 1905, describing it as 'this interesting posthumous book', if he had known that the 'unnamed friend', to whom Ross had stated in his preface that its contents were addressed, was himself. In fact Douglas was under the impression when he wrote his review that the friend was Ross and this seems to have been generally assumed at the time. Incidentally less than half of the whole letter was originally published and the title *De Profundis* was not Wilde's but was suggested by Ross's friend the literary critic E. V. Lucas, who worked for the publisher Methuen.

That Wilde was under the impression that Douglas had read the whole letter, at the time Ross states that he despatched it, appears from an incident which took place between Wilde and Douglas during the period of their temporary reunion. According to him, Douglas was reproaching Wilde about something and Wilde replied in words to this effect: 'Surely you are not bringing up against me what I wrote in prison when I was starving and half mad? You must know that I didn't mean a word of what I said.'

This brings us to the question—did Ross act honestly or disingenuously? In the first place, Ross disregarded Wilde's written instructions to send Douglas the original *De Profundis* letter, and there is no evidence that Wilde changed his instructions and asked Ross to send Douglas a typed copy instead of the manuscript—indeed the evidence, such as it is, rather points the other way. 'It is surely significant,' Douglas has written in his autobiography, 'that nowhere and at no time has Ross ever stated publicly and definitely that Wilde told him to keep the manuscript and conceal its existence from me.' Secondly, Ross, in conditions of secrecy, in 1909, presented the manuscript to the British Museum, which somewhat surprisingly accepted it. Douglas always swore that the first he knew of its existence was at the time of his libel action against Ransome three years later, when it was shown to him by Ransome's solicitors Messrs Lewis and Lewis. Afterwards he claimed that, as the manuscript was addressed to him, it should be handed over to him by the Museum.

About the time I met Douglas in 1931, or shortly afterwards, Douglas consulted Lord Hailsham, the father of the present peer, who had been Lord Chancellor and was an ex officio trustee of the Museum. Hailsham advised that the proper course was for Douglas to start a Chancery suit against the Museum for the return of the manuscript. This, Lord Hailsham said, would lead to a judicial pronouncement from the Bench, and as the Museum authorities were not at all hostile to Douglas and did not wish to keep the manuscript which was a source of embarrassment to them, Douglas would very likely get the manuscript which Lord Hailsham thought Douglas ought to have. Unfortunately for Douglas, who was still an undischarged bankrupt, the cost of the legal proceedings involved was a bar to such an action, and so Douglas was reluctantly obliged to leave the matter in *statu quo*. Thus it remained for the remainder of Douglas's life.

Last year, on 17 August 1981, Douglas's bankruptcy was annulled at the instance of his literary executor Mr Edward Colman, who had befriended him in his last years and in whose house in Lancing he died. It only took six years for Wilde's estate to become solvent, largely due to the success of his works in Germany, particularly *Salomé*. It took thirty-six years in the case of Douglas's estate, but all his creditors like Wilde's have now been paid in full through the accumulated royalties from Douglas's writings. Thus it has at last been possible, in Mr Colman's words, 'to clear an old friend's honour of the last known stain upon it.'

Although I believe that Robert Ross administered Wilde's estate honestly and well for the benefit of Wilde's two sons, who took the surname Holland, I do not think that Ross was altogether straightforward in his dealings with the *De Profundis* manuscript, disregarding Wilde's instructions that the original and not a typed copy should be sent to Douglas, then after Wilde's death publishing the work in an abbreviated form, and finally handing over the whole manuscript to the British Museum to be kept sealed up for fifty years. Had not Douglas been financially incapacitated from taking the first Lord Hailsham's advice, I am confident that he would have succeeded in recovering from the Museum what after all was a letter addressed by Wilde to himself. Having secured the annulment of Douglas's bankruptcy, perhaps his able and energetic literary executor will now turn his attention to the question of the *De Profundis* letter and take the steps for the benefit of the Douglas estate, which Lord Hailsham suggested and which Douglas was unable to follow in his lifetime.

The tragedy of Oscar Wilde and Lord Alfred Douglas is epitomised in the complete *De Profundis* letter. 'Yet from me you may have still much to gain,' Wilde wrote in the letter's concluding words. 'You came to me to learn the Pleasure of Life and the Pleasure of Art. Perhaps I am chosen to teach you something much more wonderful, the meaning of Sorrow, and its beauty.' Here, at least, I feel, Wilde spoke the truth.